AF316657

Embrace Your
Inner Peaches

Embrace Your Inner Peaches

52 *MORE* ANALOGIES *for* LEADERSHIP, COACHING *and* LIFE

Alan Heymann

Illustrations by
Lindy Russell-Heymann

Cover art by Dennis Samson

Printed in the United States of America

First Printing, 2024

ISBN 979-8-218-49645-6

Peaceful Direction
2703 Dennis Avenue
Silver Spring, MD 20902

peacefuldirection.com/book

Contents

Section 2
Presence: How We Show Up, and How We Come Across   37

Section 3
Managing Key Relationships   71

CONTENTS

Section 6
About Coaching — 165

Introduction

As a young man, I didn't set out to be a published author any more than I set out to be an executive coach or facilitator. My earlier, loftier career goals centered on being a news anchor in my hometown of Chicago. I missed the mark by about 140 miles, as it turns out. But what I gained as a small-town journalist with a state government beat was the ability to ask powerful questions and help people tell their stories. These are skills I still use every day.

My clients are usually hungry for a new understanding of their current challenges, whether they're seeking a career transition or hoping to navigate thorny relationships more effectively. I help them get to that understanding by reframing: using inquiry to help them tell a different story, or to tell the same story in a different way.

Often, that's where analogies come in. They're simple, relatable and often true. I define an analogy as a meaningful story that helps draw a connection between two ideas. In short, analogies encourage reframing by helping the leader use their imagination. They're powerful stuff. And they keep coming my way, even when I'm not looking for them. Here's one, in fact.

I once had an interview with a prospective client who bought a piece of giraffe art that she liked. Other people noticed it on the wall during video calls. Before long, her home office was filled with giraffe things that people kept buying her, or that would find her some other way — to the extent that I couldn't resist asking her about all of the giraffes when we spoke.

The same thing has happened to me with analogies. When I finished *Don't Just Have the Soup* in 2021, I kept on collecting them from coaching sessions and from the inner reaches of my own imagination. I suspect they will continue to find me in the future as well.

This collection, like the first, is one analogy for every week of the year. You can dive in like you would for a new season of your favorite streaming show and binge the whole thing at once. You can put it on your desk and enthrall your direct reports with it from time to time. And yes, you can put it in the bathroom. (It contains the word "toilet" 5 times anyway.)

Why Peaches?

The title of this book has nothing to do with fruit, despite the image on the cover.

Our titular Peaches is a cat. She's the muse of this whole collection of analogies, though I've never seen her or met her. She represents a simple idea: sometimes we hold ourselves back from releasing our full potential at work, because it seems risky or we feel like we're not enough. And sometimes when this happens, it helps to draw some inspiration from someone we admire because they don't have the same reservations. Or, if you prefer, gives less of a (choice four-letter word) about what people think of them.

You'll meet Peaches in Section 2.

Enjoy the journey!

Alan Heymann
Montgomery County, Maryland
September 2024

Inside the Leader's Mind

The leader's mind is a familiar place for me. I've carried one around myself for a couple of decades now. And it is the place I have spent most of my time during the hundreds upon hundreds of hours of one-on-one coaching I've conducted with leaders across all sectors of the economy.

It's a familiar place, but also a fascinating and complicated one.

In my experience, the mind of a successful leader does a few important things:

It reacts to circumstances both familiar and unfamiliar with curiosity, rather than assuming knowledge or jumping to conclusions.

It embarks on a nearly endless process of prioritization and deprioritization, which can seem ruthless because some people will be disappointed with the results.

It contains some kind of a system, or a strategy, for dealing with the onslaught of incoming requests and bits of information. Simply putting out fires all the time is not a system or a strategy. It's also a sure-fire recipe for burnout. (Did you see what I did there?)

It devotes at least as much energy to relationships as it does to tasks.

It recognizes that the needs of the team, the organization and the boss need to come first — often, but not always. And it is willing to invest the energy to do what I call "protecting the asset," or looking after the leader's own physical and mental health.

This section is about keeping our heads on straight in the face of increasing complexity or even in a crisis. It's also about our relationships with time, decisions and distractions.

1

The parable of the paper cut

It was a sunny weekday morning, and I was out for a run before my workday began. About a mile in, the podcast in my ears got replaced by the phone ringing. Unusual.

It was my wife. Even more unusual.

I slowed to a walk and picked up the call.

"Hi, did you see her text message?" she said, with a bit of concern.

"No, I've been out running," I replied. "Let me take a look."

Our daughter, early in her day as a ninth grader, had texted both of us a single line a few minutes earlier: "I cut myself"

My wife had texted back, asking if she was OK or needed any help. There was no reply.

"Do you want to go to the school?" she asked. "Should we call the nurse?"

I imagined two distinct scenarios. One, our teenager was sharing a bit of her school life with us — as we often asked

her to do. The same girl who carries bandages in her bag in case someone might have a need. Or two, that she was lying on the floor in a pool of her own blood, using her last bit of strength to text her parents before passing out.

I was leaning toward the first scenario being more likely, and my wife was clearly leaning toward the second. She was at work a half hour away. I could run up to the school in about 15 minutes. But I pictured the scene it would cause if a sweaty, out-of-breath, middle-aged guy panted his way into the main office at a crowded high school, and it struck me as a bit of overkill.

"I'm sure she's surrounded by people who can help her if she needs," I said. "Why don't you text her back and make sure she's OK, tell her we're happy to help if we can?"

I finished my run and continued on home, hopeful we'd made the right decision. About a half hour later, we got a reply:

"Oh no it's a small cut

Like a paper cut

Just

With my finger nail"

Sweet relief in the form of an almost-haiku. This episode did make me think about my clients, though. About how many times they might find themselves encountering a situation with a colleague, a boss, a direct report — and having an entirely different interpretation.

Is it a trauma with major blood loss? Or just a paper cut?

Coaching prompts:

- If a situation is causing you stress at work, what do you actually know about it? What are the best case and the worst case your imagination could conjure?
- What are the consequences of intervening in this situation? What are the consequences of ignoring it?

2

The time demon

Being a self-employed coach and facilitator means my activity levels can be wildly inconsistent across a month, or even a week. I might have a day with four coaching calls, followed by a day with none.

What I absolutely love: blocking out time for writing, reading and exercise.

What I don't absolutely love: sitting at my desk with an empty calendar and an empty inbox, feeling like there's nothing to do.

Nearly five years in at this writing, I'm still not used to it.

There's still a bit of residual "I should be working right now" if I'm not, during traditional work hours. You can blame capitalism, or hustle culture. I blame the time demon sitting on my shoulder.

The time demon is my shorthand for the nagging feeling that my time belongs to someone else.

Sure, I had jobs as a student where I got paid by the hour — so my time was for rent then. But in my salaried career

life, I remember the exact moment when the nagging feeling first entered my mind almost 20 years ago. The time demon had taken its seat.

It was about 9:30 in the morning on a weekday. I was working in a public-facing job for an elected official and had gone to a community event the night before. So I had decided to hang back for a bit that day, and was out walking the dog.

My cell phone rang. The boss. Said politician had a habit of leading with terror, so I instinctively prepared for the worst and answered the call. He was inquiring into my whereabouts.

"You're on my time. MY TIME!" thundered the voice into my handset. (It was my personal cell phone in an era when we paid for minutes, so it was technically my airtime. But this didn't seem quite the right moment to raise that issue.)

My dog likely had no idea why she was suddenly circling the neighborhood much faster than usual, but my chastened self high-tailed it into the office with one shoulder slightly lower than the other. The time demon was firmly planted and never went away, even at night or on weekends.

It was a leadership-by-counterexample lesson I carried forward as soon as I was leading my own teams. I told them early and often that I didn't care about the hours they kept as long as they delivered the work. And that I expected they would take time to care for their health, their dependents (human and animal), their homes, their cars, their hobbies. Please book that midday doctor's appointment, sign up for that class and go have lunch with that friend who's in from out of town, I said.

But it was a lesson I never internalized for myself. Whether I was compulsively checking my work email when I didn't need to, or sweating the example I was setting for my team when I found myself out of the office more often, I still had the time demon on my shoulder.

He doesn't appear as much as he used to. It's no longer a given that I'll always be working between the hours of 8 and 5 Monday through Friday. But it still feels, sometimes and somewhat, like I should. The time demon is like a phantom limb.

It's a hard lesson to unlearn.

Coaching prompts:

- How can you show your staff that their time is valuable — to themselves as well as to your organization?
- To what extent do you measure an employee's worth by the number of hours their butt is in a chair in the office?

3

The one-button microwave

My family spent many, many years without a microwave in the kitchen. We were doing a lot of home cooking without a lot of counter space, and I didn't feel right about rapidly heating plastic containers.

Then we had two busy adults and a growing teenager who was preparing a lot of her own food. So, about a year ago, we finally caught up with the 1980s and bought a shockingly inexpensive microwave.

It's been really convenient, especially on Thursday nights when we typically have what's left of the week's greatest hits for dinner. And, during one of those weekly bouts of reheating, I noticed something about our new appliance.

It has 19 extra buttons.

The only button any of us in the house ever uses is the one that adds 30 seconds of cooking time. If we want to heat something up for a minute, we press it twice. If we want to stop cooking, we open the door.

The microwave has other capabilities that are nice
to have, but they're not essential. It can slowly defrost
something on low power, which we've never done. It has
a clock, which needs to be reset twice a year for daylight
saving. The rest is just visual clutter.

Imagine how simple and elegant a one-button
microwave would look! And imagine not even needing an
owner's manual: you just plug it in, push the button and go.

Simplicity is such a powerful tool in product design and
in leadership. Yet we have so many elements of work that get
in the way of simplicity.

Bureaucracy. Tradition. The need to feel valuable in a role by contributing expertise.

Leaders must challenge their teams to develop simpler solutions. The path of simplicity can lead to faster innovation, lower cost and less stress for everyone involved. Ask yourself if the best solution in a given situation is actually the solution that does the least.

Sometimes, you need just a single button.

Coaching prompts:

- What is the most important objective you want to achieve in your role right now?
- How do you ensure that your team members understand and align with the essential priorities of the organization?

4

~⤳

The finish line

It was a brisk, dry Midwestern morning. Slightly warm for the season, but otherwise perfect conditions for running a half-marathon. I was running this race for the fifth time, on a flat course with great scenery and plenty of spectators.

The first nine miles seemed to fly by. I had plenty of energy and great music. I was dressed properly. My legs almost knew what to do without any signal from my brain. We saw classic old Victorian houses, early brunch-goers and much of a college campus.

I powered through the next 3-1/2 miles, which were tougher. I had a bit of fatigue. We ran up a couple of hills. I stopped for water a couple of times. And then I hit what would turn out to be the hardest point in the race for me.

I had all of a half-mile to go. I knew this because the course was basically a loop, and we were near where we started. I was also using a run tracker. It would all be over in

less than five minutes, barely enough time for a song or two on my running mix.

I knew all of this intellectually, but not physically. Because I couldn't see the finish line.

The course had changed since the last time I ran it, so we had to make a quick turn before the end. The finish line wasn't visible until the last block or two of the race. Which might has well have been another three miles.

I pushed, I powered, I persevered. I got my medal and my margarita. I took an epic nap and ate a large meal. But I kept thinking about how I felt like the race was never going to end.

We're not meant to run at race pace during all of our training runs, and we're not meant to run 16 miles when we've trained for 13.1. At some point, the body has to stop moving.

This is also how we work.

We can rev ourselves up for the final stretch to meet a deadline: the book is published, Election Day passes, the app update goes live. But what if the finish line isn't that obvious?

When you're in emergency medicine, or disaster response, or government, the work is never actually done.

That's where leaders make the difference. When you're in charge, it's up to you to at least lay down the mile markers. The milestones that lead to success are up to you. And you know the difference between the effort you can reasonably expect from a peak performer and the effort that will lead to burnout.

Try a mini finish line, or a series of them. Build in a rest cycle. Repeat.

Coaching prompts:

- How might you help your team understand what completion looks like, or when they've achieved it?
- What might you do to honor the milestone, beyond acknowledgment and heading straight back to work?

5

The smoke alarm

The client was rounding the corner on an insight. She needed to be more visible to the members of a particular team under her command. To learn more about their day-to-day, yes, and to show that upper management was a group of actual human beings as well. While on the precipice of this aha moment, my client was mid-sentence, and…

BEEP! BEEP! BEEP!
BEEP! BEEP! BEEP!

As my teen daughter would say, "What the literal heck?"

It was the smoke alarm in my home office, taking an opportunity to interrupt my client and terrify my dog. I quickly excused myself. Verified that my house was not, in fact, on fire. Removed the offending cylinder from the ceiling and placed it outside. Then invited the client to continue.

This happened once more the next day, during a different session with a different client. I got annoyed, then I got curious. It's a 2-year-old smoke detector with a 10-year

battery in it. None of its neighboring alarms had gone off. I looked at the instructions, blew a little potential dust out of the openings, and put it back on the ceiling. Hasn't happened since.

And then I realized there's probably a lesson here, for my clients and for me.

Suppose there's an interruption in your usual thinking. It's loud, and persistent, and you're annoyed. If you're the sort of person who doesn't usually get annoyed, you'll probably find yourself annoyed by the annoyance. Yet this is probably a signal that something's up.

What is it that's causing you to stick on this particular

conversation, or issue, or colleague? Why won't the annoyance in your head let up?

Maybe something's seriously wrong here, and you're receiving an early warning signal. But if it isn't a house fire, you could be in the midst of conditions that are causing your warning system to trigger too easily. Showing up for work tired, stressed or hungry could be the dust in the air that sets off the alarm.

During the first interrupted coaching session, my first impulse wasn't the right one. It would take just a few seconds to smash the smoke detector with a hammer, ending the offensive beeping and allowing my client to continue her story. But then I'd be unprotected in the event of an actual fire.

Instead, the solution was to get curious.

Coaching prompts:

- What does your early-warning system feel like in your body? When do you first notice it?
- How do you tell the difference between a real crisis and a false alarm?

6

When debate prep is over

This book is coming into the world during a presidential election year, and I love me a presidential debate. I've loved them for as long as I can remember, certainly long before a debate vastly changed the trajectory of the 2024 race.

I know one's ability to perform in a debate doesn't strongly predict one's ability to govern. I know debates are performative, and the introvert in me winces when a lesser-known candidate in a crowded primary must grasp for microphone time. But I look at it like the Olympics of the political arena: those who survive a brutal process and make it to the very top must display their skills for an audience of millions.

From memoirs and history books, I know that the process of preparing a candidate for a debate is a big project involving many, many people. There are briefing books, mock run-throughs, video critiques and the like. And I like

to imagine that a lot of the candidate's potential for success comes from a single, pivotal moment in the process.

The moment of "enough."

There has to be a moment when the candidate's brain is full enough of facts and figures. When they've had enough jousting with the person impersonating their opponent. When they've watched themselves on camera and critiqued their own performance enough. They need a breath, they need some rest, maybe some time to themselves.

I'm imagining that the moment arrives differently depending on the style of the candidate. Is it someone who continued cramming facts and figures on the walk over to an exam in college, or someone who stopped studying the night before and got a good sleep beforehand? Does the person believe there is such a thing as over-preparation? Woe to the candidate who waves the advisers away and insists they can perform without any help.

But at some point, whether it's a day earlier or right before the awkward handshake on stage, the prep must end.

And this isn't an idea reserved for those who are seeking the highest office in the land.

The "enough" moment happens for every leader before every pivotal meeting. It could be a job interview, a presentation before the board, a pitch for a key investor. My gentle encouragement here is to not let the moment pass you by, by rushing from one meeting into the next.

Instead, pause.

Remember that you've read and seen and heard enough. That you are enough.

Coaching prompts:

- When preparing for a critical meeting, what would you do with a bit of time and space to yourself before the meeting begins?
- How do you recognize that you've reached a saturation point, and cannot absorb any more information on a topic or set of topics?

7

The uninvited houseguest

My clients bring their daily work challenges into coaching sessions, and we often journey into discussing elements of their personalities that don't seem to be serving them. Imposter phenomenon. Anxiety.* People pleasing.

Sometimes we have an element of how we show up in the world and dislike that element deeply. It almost feels like having an unwanted guest who's been living in your head for years. It's frustrating, and it's also nearly impossible to turn off.

I usually start conversations like this by asking the client to consider some gratitude for whatever it is that's making them uncomfortable. There is often a positive element in the origin story. Imposter phenomenon can protect us from taking unnecessary risks. Anxiety can drive creativity and achievement. People pleasing can help us develop social skills.

The gratitude piece can take awhile. It's hard to be thankful for something when you're mad at it. But the client typically comes around after some thought and dialogue.

I then ask the client to name this unwanted element. Not a generic name, like the Fear or Ennui of the "Inside Out" movies. An actual person's name. One client named her anxiety Suzy. Another named his people pleasing Fred. With the name, I ask them to imagine how this character would look.

The next step is to think of the character as just one of several whose points of view are part of the conversation — even though it's dominating the conversation right now.

Think Abraham Lincoln's contentious cabinet in *Team of Rivals.*

Lastly, I invite the client to bring it all together into a short conversation with their character. Something along these lines:

"Fred, I understand your point of view. Thank you for sharing it, and for doing such hard work to protect me over all these years. I hear you, and I've decided to go in a different direction. You can feel free to take a seat quietly now, or you may leave the room."

It's a quick reframe that depersonalizes the situation and reduces its magnitude. My client is then free to invoke a similar dialogue the next time an unwanted houseguest shows up for dinner in their head.

Coaching prompts:

- In what way might an unwanted feeling have served you well in the past?
- How might you balance this feeling against others that could be more useful right now?

By "anxiety," I'm referring to the everyday, low-grade kind, not a clinical anxiety disorder. Coaches aren't mental health professionals, and we're not licensed or trained to help treat the latter. But we do know where the dividing line tends to be between the two, and we will suggest that a client seek other support when needed.

8

Allergy shots

Consider the allergy shot. A little more than a hundred years ago, a couple of scientists figured out that injecting a patient with a little bit of a thing eventually cures the patient of being allergic to that thing.

At first glance, the idea of the allergy shot sounds bonkers to me. Someone's suffering from an allergy to grass, and you decide to try to help them by injecting them with grass? I'd be searching for some kind of anti-grass instead. But then again, there are many really, really good reasons that nobody pays me to come up with scientific discoveries.

Mental health has a similar concept with exposure therapy. Start with a picture of a snake. A video might be next. Then we're looking at a safely-enclosed live snake from across the room. Eventually we might be petting a snake that's harmless to humans, and our ophidiophobia is on its way to being a thing of the past.

Both ideas center on strengthening the immune system, whether physical or mental. But this work isn't confined to

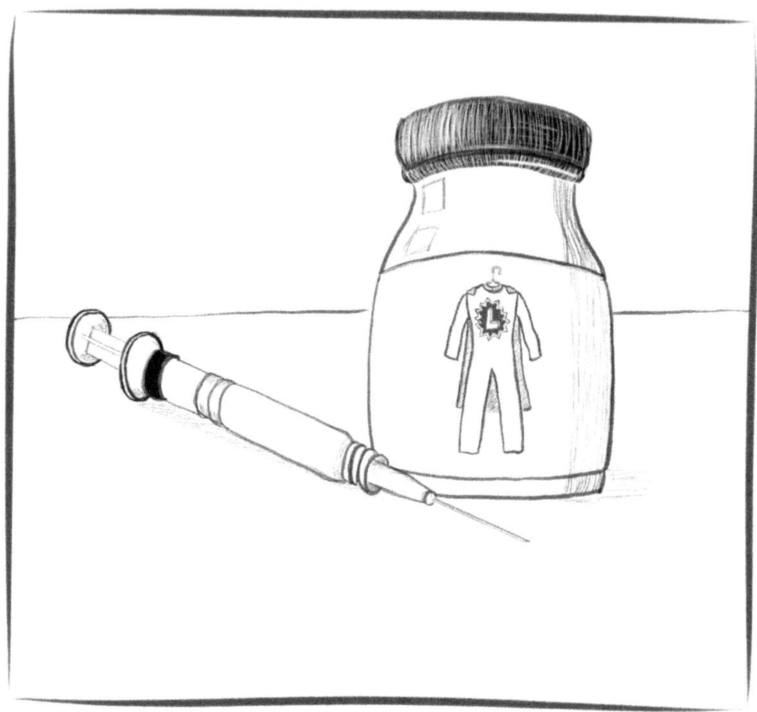

medicine and psychotherapy. Leaders do it, too. The best leaders are always looking for ways to help people in their chains of command grow by leaving their comfort zones.

This means introducing just a little bit of what hurts. Shahmeen Sadiq of Anjali Leadership, a fabulous mentor coach, pointed this idea out to me. I've been referring to it in my head ever since as the "leadership allergy shot."

If you've ever been assigned to a project that's a little outside your comfort zone because someone thought you could do it… you've had a leadership allergy shot.

If you've asked a member of your team to present to the senior leadership on their work, instead of giving that presentation yourself, because you wanted that person to step up a little and be visible… you've given a leadership allergy shot.

Shahmeen recently helped me surface the idea that I'm not very comfortable asking for referrals — even though I run a referral-based business. So I nudged myself by contacting just a couple of people in my network to ask them. A self-inflicted leadership allergy shot. And I didn't even have to feel a pin prick or get sleepy afterward.

Coaching prompts:

- If you think of an aspect of leadership that makes you very uncomfortable, what is the smallest action you could take to get closer to it?
- What can you do to nudge a member of your team toward their area of discomfort?

9

The perfect bottle of wine

My client and I were already spending a second session on a decision she was finding especially troubling. Indecision wasn't typically an issue for her. Something was different here. Too many moving parts, too many people potentially affected.

I asked her to think about what "good enough" might look like here, about reaching a point when it was time to stop deliberating and move on.

"I guess it's like trying to bring a bottle of wine to a friend's house," she said.

Naturally, I needed to hear more.

"You've gone to the corner market or the liquor store to buy a bottle," she continued. "And you can walk up and down the aisles trying to spot labels you recognize or reading the little reviews they post. Or you can realize you need to make a decision within 5 minutes or you're going to be late for dinner."

I realized my client was talking about satisficing, a concept that's many decades old and still doesn't roll off the tongue. The basic idea: if you have infinite time and resources, you might be able to make a hypothetically better decision. If you don't, you have to pick something that's good enough and move on.

Of course, this happens all the time at work. Leaders are constantly required to make decisions with barely sufficient information and little if any time to spare.

"What's the risk in the wine scenario?" I asked. "If the one you bring ends up being a dud?"

"Not likely," she replied. "I know a little bit about wine, so I'm relying on experience and instinct when I buy it. Worst case, my friend and I have a laugh about it and don't choose the same bottle again next time."

Cheers.

Coaching prompts:

- What is potentially at risk if you feel like you're close to the right decision, but you're putting off finalizing it?
- When might having limited time actually help you make a better decision?

10

The Emperor

It was midway through elementary school when I entered the "Star Wars" universe via watching "Return of the Jedi" on the big screen. I was amassing a collection of vehicles and action figures as fast as my allowance (and holidays and birthdays) would allow. And then I set my sights on a rare prize: the Emperor.

The tiny plastic version of this ultimate ruler of an evil empire wasn't on sale in stores. To receive it, I'd have to fill out the card on the back of another action figure package and send it off in the mail.

I remember dutifully taping $3.98, including the pennies, to that card. With a 20-cent stamp, off it went to Kenner Products in Cincinnati. All I had to do was wait 6 to 8 weeks for the Emperor to arrive.

Exactly 5 weeks later, I began stationing myself at the end of the driveway every weekday afternoon to wait for the mail. Friends would ask me at school the next day, "Is it here yet?" "Not yet," I'd reply.

The little box did come in the mail at some point. Inside was a figure of a wrinkly old man whose limbs couldn't move as much as the others in my collection. I probably brought him to school to show him off. Back at home, he took his place in the re-enacted space fantasies of the day, until I eventually lost interest in "Star Wars" and moved on.

Forty years later, that hunk of molded resin would be worth a whole lot of money if I still had it. What I have instead is appreciation for the anticipation of the thing. It was special because it was rare, and because it took a long time to get to me.

Today, if I decide I need a new bath rug, I can order it in seconds and have it arrive at my doorstep in a few hours. It feels like using The Force, even though I know it's destructive to small business and the environment. And of course, I never really *need* a bath rug within hours.

I think a lot about the effect of this immediacy in leadership. If we've been conditioned to anticipate every result quickly, we may not be developing the resilience we need to stick through obstacles, delays and other challenges. It's often on us to demonstrate patience in the face of disappointment. It also feels great to celebrate an accomplishment that was a long time in the making.

The little boy sitting at the end of the driveway may have been on to something after all.

Coaching prompts:

- What is the role of anticipation when it comes to things that bring you joy?
- What would happen if you intentionally took the long way in getting somewhere, or in getting something done?

11

Tapper

My mind wandered back recently to a video game I used to play 40 years ago or so. I was thinking about it because I now realize it explains how I've worked during most of my career.

The game was centered on a bar room, and it was called Tapper. (The creators renamed it Root Beer Tapper amid concerns about corrupting young minds, but I digress.) Your job as the bartender was to do two things: slide frosty, full mugs across the bar to thirsty patrons, and collect the empty mugs when patrons slide them back.

Do this enough times, and you move on to the next level. It sounds simple enough when the game starts out slowly, but it's very easy to fall behind.

Fail to serve a patron fast enough, serve a full mug to a patron who's not ready, or let an empty mug fall to the floor without catching it? You lose a round and have to start over. When you lose three rounds, the game is done.

For extra effect, the failure would come along with the primitive, digitized sound of breaking glass. Or the sight of an angry patron physically tossing you out of the bar.

I was never a bartender. But I've been Tapper during most of the jobs I've had. My patrons were constituents when I worked in local government. Or members of the media. Or my bosses and staff.

I've been afraid to let things drop, or to forget something or someone.

I've been in a hurry to complete the task and move on to the next one.

I've been taking on the urgency of others as my own.

What I've eventually learned, and have been much slower to embody, is this: some ideas need time and space to breathe. Being the fastest to respond or execute doesn't automatically make one a better employee.

Sometimes the patron will have to wait for the beer. And some glasses need to drop to the ground and shatter. But that doesn't necessarily mean you're out of the game.

Coaching prompts:

- If you are able to pause for a breath or zoom out a level, is the urgency of a given task as high as the person requesting it says it is?
- In what way might delaying execution on something present an advantage?

Presence: How We Show Up, and How We Come Across

Ah, the elusive "executive presence."

Many a client wishes to improve, or expand, this. Perhaps their boss told them to work on it. Their ideas aren't coming across as clearly as they'd like. Or they don't fit into the typically outgoing, dominant, extroverted older white male leadership model and don't want to pretend to be someone they're not.

We've crossed an important threshold as a society, and we're not going back to the days when people who look like me ran everything everywhere. But progress has been frustratingly slow. In 2023, for the first time, more CEOs of S&P 500 companies were people who identified as women than were people who identified as men named John.

Whether you tick nearly every privilege box like the Johns and I do, or belong to a group that's been historically underrepresented in Western leadership, presence shows up differently for everyone.

Also true: no coach can give you more, better or different presence. It is, on the other hand, something you can develop. And you know it when you see it.

My best example of presence comes from someone I had the good fortune to meet in 2005: His Holiness the XIV Dalai Lama. Our conversation was no more than a few seconds long. Yet in that time, leaning down to hear him, my hand in his, I felt like we were the only two people in the entire world.

In short, I could see that he was truly, fully, wonderfully present during our brief encounter.

I believe presence starts with the quality of being present. I also believe we're more surrounded than ever with distractions that pull us away from this very thing.

Presence also starts with intention. We have a lot more control over how we show up and how we come across when we're thinking about it clearly.

Are you ready to meet Peaches now?

12

Your inner Peaches

It was an audio-only coaching call, the client an executive who still felt fairly new in her role. She was nervous about an important presentation with board members and other executives the next day. I couldn't see the worry on her face, but I could hear it in her voice.

This extremely educated, extremely successful person was becoming mired in self doubt. What if they don't think I'm good enough for this job? Or not smart enough?

We talked about preparation, about breath work, about pre-performance rituals.

Then my mind started to wander a little bit toward the unfair pressure women tend to face in leadership. In short, it's a fair bet they'll be tagged as "too something" by the men in their working world. But I quickly snapped back into the present moment when my client… laughed. Out loud.

"What's funny?" I asked.

"Oh, I just looked over at my bed, as we're sitting here talking about ways for me to relax, and Peaches is all

sprawled out upside down, without a care in the world," she said.

I couldn't see Peaches, but I've had cats and could easily picture the scene. A yawning bundle of lazy fur, with everything right out there on display for the world. At first blush, another distraction of working from home.

But as I say, I've had cats before. And if there's one thing I know about cats, it's that I've never come across another living creature that cares *less* about humanity's opinion of them.

I shared this observation with my client, and asked, "What would it be like for you to embrace your inner Peaches before that presentation?"

She chuckled again, and said this would probably help her focus less on the others in the audience and more on her content and delivery.

The presentation was a success. And this was the first time I'd offered a client the idea of changing their leadership mindset by conjuring the image of cat genitals. I wonder if it will be the last.

Coaching prompts:

- When giving a presentation, when is it helpful to keep the audience in mind? When is it helpful to let the audience go?
- If you imagined yourself fearless and unconcerned with the opinions of others, how would you describe that feeling?

13

You never know who's having the salad

I've been on a plant-based diet for more than two decades. During that time, I feel so fortunate that the available dining options have exploded. Gone are the days of my surrendering to the soggy French fries while everyone around is enjoying their meal.

So here's a party trick I like to roll out sometimes at restaurants.

If I'm dining with a friend or colleague who identifies as female, the odds are pretty good that she eats differently than I do. I don't consume animal products, but most people do.

"Watch this," I'll say, as the person who brings our meal out from the kitchen turns out to not be the person who took our orders.

The food runner prepares to lay down that turkey burger in front of me. And I'll explain that I actually had the tofu. Or we'll just switch plates after they're both on the table.

It happens almost without fail. I'm the larger, more masculine diner. So the heartier, meatier meal must be mine, right?

What I'll call the implicit vegan bias shows up in other ways, including at work.

Yes, I'm over six feet tall and over 200 pounds, and I'm a white man with a deep voice. And yes, I more than occasionally make my living standing in front of groups of people. But I'm also an introvert. I'm never the first person to speak when I'm part of the group. I often feel socially awkward.

These elements of my presence aren't as obvious. They catch people by surprise, especially when those people have different expectations of me.

Much like my fondness for salad.

Coaching prompts:

- In what ways have you made a judgment about someone before they step into the room? Before they speak?
- What would happen if you tried on the opposite of your original assumption?

(Think of this as the sequel to Don't just have the soup, the analogy that inspired my last book.)

14

The introvert batteries

Picture someone in professional dress, sitting on the floor in an airport, closely tethered to a wall outlet by a tiny cable. There's nothing unusual about this sight today, but it was quite unfamiliar just a generation ago.

A generation ago, we also knew little of how the introverted mind actually works.

Think of everything our smartphones do for us. (Too much, certainly, but that's a topic for another day.) There comes a point where no matter how important the call or how interesting the TikTok video, the battery's just too empty to continue.

And so it is with my own introvert batteries. They're the measure of my capacity for social interaction. I'm drawn to certain people and certain situations, and can enjoy myself with these more than almost anywhere else in life. But there comes a point when I'm just… done.

It's not about enjoyment. I love my work. I get more joy from serving my clients, from engaging with them, than I've

had from any other work I've done in my career. It's also work that requires a tremendous amount of energy — energy I must manage carefully if I'm going to succeed.

So I've come to realize that the self-aware introvert knows where the juice is going, and how to manage it or bring it back.

Creating conditions to preserve energy

Think of this as power-saving mode on a smartphone. You want to do what you can to make sure the battery lasts the whole day before you can plug it in again. Here's how I do it:

Environment. Working for myself, by myself, at home in a quiet suburb is a tremendous privilege. It also suits me perfectly. It allows me to build social interaction into my workday instead of trying to filter it out. I'm on teams because I want to be, not because I have to be.

Quantity. I keep my coaching sessions to 4 a day, 5 at a maximum. My calendar could probably tolerate a lot more, but what good is a coach with low energy?

Spacing. I try to give myself a few minutes between calls to gather my thoughts, move a little, use the bathroom or grab food and drink.

Restoring energy

Here's how I recharge. You can't have a cell phone without a charger and a cable (or some kind of wireless setup). I've come to rely on two essential recharging elements just as much — not for survival, but for the sake of my mental health and my effectiveness in work:

Silence. During the workday, I'm often hearing my computer fan, a chirping bird, an occasional dog bark and little else. I'm a light sleeper and travel with silicone earplugs. Silence is restorative for me. When I end a workday feeling like I'm full of other people's words, I power back up with quiet.

Solitude. If I'm feeling socially drained at home and need a quick power-up, I take the dog out for a pee or go out and check the mailbox. If I need a longer break, I'll put on a yoga video or work on a jigsaw puzzle until my batteries feel more charged again. Out in the world, a bathroom break or drink refill is a wonderful pause. And I always build in plenty of breaks when I'm working with groups, so I can recharge along with my fellow introverts.

Coaching prompts:

- Which situations in life, and which people, give you energy? Which of these come with an energy cost?
- What do you do to preserve and recover your energy?

15

Spinach in my teeth, revisited

My last book had an analogy called "Spinach in my teeth," which was about the often difficult choice to say something that someone may not want to hear. I shared the story of letting a friend walk around with a stray nose hair rather than bringing it up with him.

The analogy has been a hit with audiences of coaches and leaders when I've taken it on the road. I got good responses when I sent it out to my email list, including one that is well worth some real estate here.

Let's just say someone had "spinach in their teeth" and I decided to treat them the way I would want to be treated. I let them know. I also offered some suggestions on how to prevent the spinach from getting stuck in the first place.

As you may be guessing, it was not taken well. I was deemed to be too "critical." There is a nuance to giving feedback that makes people hesitant because of the potential for a negative interaction.

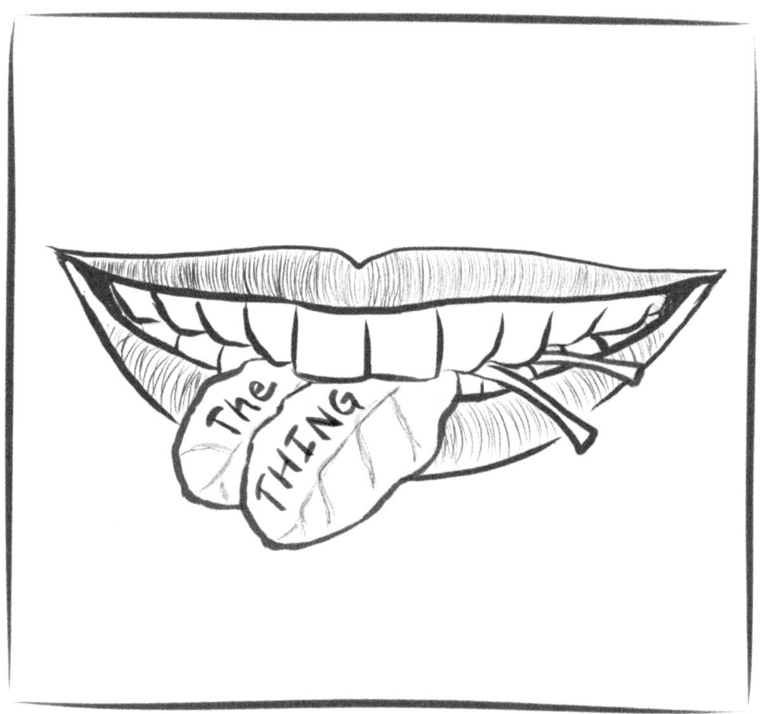

For a bit of additional context, the person who sent this is a longtime client who is also a Black woman. I'm quite certain she has been accused of being "too much" this, or "not enough" that, a lot more often than I have. Her note helped me personalize the idea that not all senders and recipients of feedback are the same.

When I first wrote about the spinach in 2021, I was thinking about situations where sharing constructive feedback would benefit the recipient, and would improve the relationship over time. I was also thinking about people who are generally inclined to say The Thing, and people who are generally hesitant.

I wasn't thinking about people who might feel the need to perform a calculation every time before they decide to say The Thing. It's a calculation about whether speaking up is worth a potential hit to their reputation. Or possibly reflecting in a certain way on their entire race, gender, sexual orientation or some combination of these.

So not every moment is a spinach moment for every person. Some of us carry around more burdens than others, and the burden of being someone else's mirror is just a lot to handle.

Sometimes a bit of spinach is just a bit of spinach. And sometimes it's a whole lot more.

Coaching prompts:

- As you weigh the possibility of voicing some critical feedback, what is the potential cost to your reputation or relationship? What is the potential benefit?
- Do others tend to look to you to say the uncomfortable thing? Why or why not?

16

The salesperson

I can't think of sales without thinking of Alec Baldwin's iconic motivational speech in "Glengarry Glen Ross":
"First prize is a Cadillac Eldorado.
Second prize is a set of steak knives.
Third prize is you're fired."

I know this a dramatic oversimplification. I know the work of sales isn't all about quotas and pressure tactics. I know the business-to-business economy — in which I'm an active participant — would not exist if not for people servicing the accounts of other people through relationships and trust.

At its best, sales is a way of connecting people with what they want when they want it. At its worst, it's manipulative, invasive, undesired.

And yet, even as a proud introvert with a profound distaste for the sales-y side of sales, I have come to a realization that might make you as uncomfortable as it makes me.

It is impossible to become a leader or succeed as a leader without being involved in sales.

We are all in sales. And the product is us.

In an interview for a promotion, we are selling our prospective employer on the idea of us as a good fit for a leadership role. We are asking them to imagine what their life would be like with us in the position we're seeking. We are sharing the benefits, the approach, the perspective we would bring to their team.

In leadership, we must become more comfortable with claiming credit for the work of our teams. This involves directing the work and selling it. Doing the selling part brings visibility to the part of the organization we lead, illustrating its value for others. Without this visibility, it will be harder for us to get the support we need from upper management or to compete for scarce resources.

Just waiting until someone notices that we're absolutely crushing it… is not good strategy. It's time to sell the value of your work.

Even if you've never spent a minute doing external business development, and even if your team is the farthest away from sales on the org chart, you are in sales.

Coaching prompts:

- What are some ways you can authentically call attention to your work and that of your team?
- Who are the key internal customers who need to hear this message the most?

17

CNN host, or dissertation author?

I'm fond of telling people I was a journalism major in college and worked in communications for more than two decades, which makes me an expert in precisely nothing. I say this to potential clients as a way to let them know I'm not an expert in delegation, or managing up, or whatever issues they're bringing into the realm of coaching. I do tend to know who those experts are, and I can guide the clients to them.

What I learned years ago during my brief time in television is that expertise and credibility are not the same thing. It's easy to confuse the two because you need a bit of both to succeed in front of an audience. I've had a fair number of clients tell me they don't feel like they have enough expertise on a topic to be comfortable owning it. I ask them to think about the distinction between expertise and credibility, and what the situation demands.

For an example of how expertise and credibility work, let's turn to CNN. Seriously. I've never been a big consumer of cable news — I don't have a television in my house, so I'll catch a glimpse infrequently in an airport or a doctor's office. And I know many of society's ills can be traced to talking heads screaming misinformation at each other. But the format can give us a useful example.

Imagine we have a topic in the news. The president has hired a new chief of staff, and CNN is doing a segment with the author of a doctoral dissertation about presidential chiefs of staff.

The host knows the audience. The host's job is to connect the author to that audience. The host must be conversant in the subject and have great questions to frame the conversation in a way that informs and inspires the audience. But they don't have to be the expert. High credibility, lower expertise.

The author's job is to get the message out according to the contours of the interview. The author shares not all of what they know on the topic, but a small sampling of it. The author must be well-spoken and knowledgeable. But they don't have to frame the conversation or know the audience. High expertise, lower credibility.

Both participants in the interview need expertise and credibility, but at different levels because they have different roles.

So, the next time you're giving a presentation, delivering a briefing or facilitating a meeting, are you the host or the author?

Coaching prompts:

- What level of expertise does your audience expect in this situation?
- In what ways might expertise get in the way of your ability to deliver a message?

18

The court of appeals

My client was getting bogged down in too many petty squabbles on her team. People who didn't even report directly to her would bring her their issues, and she would listen somewhat patiently while trying not to focus on everything else that needed her attention.

She was an approachable leader whose "door is always open" attitude kept her well connected to her staff. It also kept her working nights and weekends because she felt like she couldn't catch a break.

It feels good to help others solve their problems, and it feels good to be needed. I suspected her receptiveness had opened her up to too much of a good thing. Knowing we'd both gone to law school at some point, I decided to tee up an analogy.

"What if you're supposed to be the court of appeals?" I asked.

Her facial expression was the perfect blend of "I'm not sure what you're talking about" and "Please, continue." I

tend to see this a lot on my clients' faces, so I took it as an invitation to explain more.

A court of appeals is where you go if you have legal grounds to try to overturn what happened in a lower court. Not every party in every trial has the right to an appeal, and the courts don't have to hear every case where an appeal is optional.

Appeals courts work differently, too. They don't usually conduct trials, and they rarely allow new evidence into the record. Their job is mostly to review what happened in the trial court.

None of this happens until the work of the trial court — the ground floor of the judicial system — is done.

I wondered if my client wasn't letting her front-line supervisors do the work of the trial court, so her people were coming to her directly instead. When I asked her to imagine what a different scenario might look like, she offered that she could send someone back to their direct boss first.

She didn't really know the next step yet. Would it be "keep me posted," or "let me know how else I can help," or that she didn't want to get involved again at all, except for a special set of circumstances.

But she was committed to trying to figure it out.

Coaching prompts:

- When are you finding yourself drawn into disputes or discussions where you don't feel like your presence is necessary?
- In what ways might it hold your team back if you give them too much access to you?

19

Be Santa Claus

I've long thought that successful leadership requires subtraction as well as addition. As you're adding things like:

- responsibilities
- direct reports
- budget authority

You need to let go of things like:

- operational details
- technical expertise
- doing the thing

The distinction between adding and subtracting catches a lot of leaders by surprise, and it ends up in a lot of my coaching conversations. And so it was with a client who had

decades of experience and tended to lead with a lot of heart. He came into a session frustrated by his seeming inability to connect with a team he had recently inherited.

He had done everything he knew how to do, but it wasn't working. I wondered out loud if he might be doing too much.

My question stopped the conversation cold, which is a scary record scratch of a moment for a coach. I leaned into the silence until he invited me to say more.

"Think about Santa Claus," I said. "Kids love him because he brings them presents. He fulfills their wishes. He is all about good things."

The client nodded, looking slightly curious.

"But I think Santa Claus is special because he only comes once a year," I continued. "Imagine he shows up every night and brings you things like new socks, or a fresh tube of toothpaste. He's asked you what you want so many times that you're making things up, because you're out of ideas. Meanwhile, your parents are getting upset because they can't buy milk and cookies fast enough, and they're having to clean up soot around the chimney every night."

"The novelty would wear out pretty fast, I think," said my client.

This time, I nodded.

"So you're saying I should be more like Santa Claus?" he asked.

I responded that I wasn't saying he should do anything at all — merely wondering if it might be time to try experimenting with the opposite approach to what he had been doing.

Like many aspects of leadership, face time is a balancing act. I've personally been in situations where I couldn't get enough of the boss's attention when I felt I really needed it. In reaction to feeling like I must've been on the naughty list, I may have made myself too available as a leader at times.

I just hope nobody felt compelled to bring me cookies.

Coaching prompts:

- What do you do to remain visible and available to your direct reports? How would you know if you had overstayed your welcome?
- In what ways might it empower your staff if you reduce their access to your time and attention?

20

The red nose

When I met him for the first time, the client looked like he fit the profile. Federal employee. Decades of experience in law enforcement. Uniform. With a bald head, a large frame and a powerful handshake.

I wasn't intimidated, exactly. Though I will say he got my attention.

It turns out first impressions were exactly what he wanted to discuss in coaching. He had recently landed a new assignment in an unfamiliar office. He saw himself as a person who had a big heart, in an environment not known for caring. He did care. He wanted to look after his team, for them to trust him and confide in him.

But he had enough self-awareness to know how he came across to people who didn't know him well, and he wanted to soften the impact.

We talked through examples of people he knows, and why he considers them approachable and kind. One thing

they had in common was an element of silliness. Of not taking themselves too seriously.

With his permission, I decided to take my client through a small thought experiment.

"What would happen if you took on a completely silly element in your appearance," I asked, "like a red clown nose?"

He looked puzzled. "You want me to wear a red clown nose to the office?"

"Not exactly," I replied. The idea I had in mind was slightly different: for him to put himself into a team or group setting while *imagining* he was wearing a red clown nose. That something might change in the way he interacted with others if he took himself less seriously, and this enabled them to take him less seriously.

His reaction included a facial expression that, if I'm being honest, was a little hard to read. But he did agree to try on an imaginary red clown nose at the office holiday party a couple of weeks later.

At the party, it turns out my client was able to have several engaging conversations with staffers about their plans for the holiday. It was a tentative first step toward building the trust he was seeking. And he never had to worry about an actual red nose falling into the punch bowl.

Coaching prompts:

- In what ways might the impression you make on others be shaped by your impression of yourself?
- What attributes would you like to see more of in yourself, and what attributes would you like to see less of? What might change as a result?

21

The all-you-can-eat buffet

My client was frustrated because his efforts weren't leading to a promotion. Meanwhile, his day was so broken into fragments that he couldn't focus on leading the longer-term initiatives or thinking the bigger thoughts.

I had a hunch.

"What percentage of meeting requests would you say you accept?" I asked.

"As close to a hundred as possible," he replied.

As I encouraged my client to think about whether this setup was working for him, I thought back to a time in my own career as a leader.

I once sat on an executive team with a colleague who was never available. I don't mean you couldn't meet with him. I mean his schedule, in Outlook, was always a monolith of unavailability. To get on his calendar, you needed to make a specific request directly to him — or to his assistant.

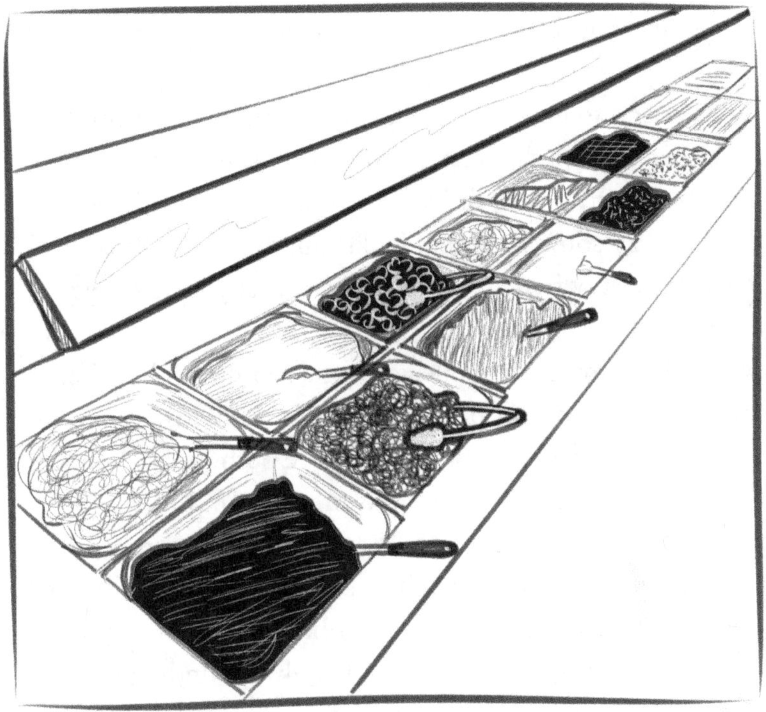

At the time, I found this profoundly irritating. It struck me as a power play, a statement that his time was always more valuable than everyone else's. Of course, I later realized that he was exactly right. The wisdom didn't hit me until I became a coach and needed to tightly manage the time I have available for clients.

That's when I found myself wondering when and how it became the norm for every unused block of time in the workweek to be available to everyone else.

Why on earth are we letting others treat our schedules like an all-you-can-eat buffet, where every open block of time has a spoon or a pair of tongs sticking out? That everyone can just reach in and grab whatever they think they need?

We tend to be pretty careless with abundance. I think it's human nature that comes from our distant ancestors not knowing exactly when or where the next meal would come. Why not try something that looks unfamiliar or pile on a few more soggy french fries? It doesn't cost you anything more.

Back to my former colleague for a moment. His schedule wasn't a buffet — far from it. In fact, you couldn't even get into the restaurant without advance permission. Every morsel of food on every plate was precious, and you had to make careful choices as a result. You'd savor the experience.

And we always did. Much as I chafed at the scheduling inconvenience more than once — I have an impatient streak about these things — I do remember always finding him kind, thoughtful and fully present during those few meetings I managed to land.

Coaching prompts:

- Are others treating your time, energy and attention as the limited and valuable resources they are?
- What benefits might you realize from being less available?

Managing Key Relationships

Nobody leads an organization, or a team, in a vacuum. From the Fortune 50 CEO who must contend with regulators, investors and thousands of employees, to the independent business owner who has clients and frequent collaborators on the brain, we've all got stakeholders.

Managing the relationships with those stakeholders — call it managing up, down and sideways — is an indisputable building block of effective leadership. Show me a boss who says "I'm not a people person" or gets pulled into "so many conversations that I can't do my real job," and I'll show you someone who's missing the point.

The conversations *are* the real job.

It should be no surprise that much of what awaits you in this section centers on communication. It's where I spent the bulk of my career before launching my business, and it's where you'll find the most challenge and opportunity in managing relationships.

Please enjoy your visit to the press conference, the doctor's office and the car dealership.

22

⤳

The bank of
relationship capital

When I ran communications for a water utility, I used to talk about a "reservoir of goodwill" with customers, the press and other key players. (Did you see what I did there, with water and reservoir? Anyway…) The basic idea: the organization sometimes did things that increased the happiness and understanding of stakeholders, and sometimes did things that would do the exact opposite.

Hence the reservoir. We'd fill it up with outreach events, infrastructure upgrades that solved long-standing flooding problems and the like. We'd drain it with rate increases and service outages that were unfortunate but necessary.

Years later, I think leaders can operate in a very similar way with their key stakeholders. I've asked clients to imagine a bank account full of relationship capital.

My people pleasers might build up a giant cushion of savings over a period of years, not realizing they can afford to spend it in service of a decision that will cause short-term pain for the long-term good. Picture a leader who's a great listener, has built a lot of trust with the team and nicely balances the employee's career aspirations with the organization's financial interests. This person has plenty to spare in their credibility bank account. When the time comes for that new direction or long-postponed reorg, they can spend almost lavishly and the team will follow along.

On the other hand, leaders with the opposite approach will face nothing but challenges in living from credibility paycheck to credibility paycheck. Their relationships will be transactional, as they find themselves in the business of trading favors to get to success. It's extremely difficult to bring people along with you in service of a new vision when you haven't earned enough credibility to sway them. If your boss is well-regarded, they might be able to lend you some relationship capital. But going into credibility debt won't work in the long term.

Coaching prompts:

- How much credibility have you earned with your boss, your team and other key stakeholders while you've been in your position?
- Have you been reluctant to spend this credibility? Or too eager to do so? For what purpose?

23

The boss's user manual

Any new product you bring into your life needs to answer a basic question: how do I get this thing, or this collection of pieces of a thing, to do what I bought it to do? It could be a vacuum cleaner, a bag of frozen vegetables or a dining room table.

There's always a how-to list. Instructions for assembly, instructions for use, maybe even instructions for how long to wait before you'll know the thing is working.

I believe new bosses should be like vacuum cleaners or frozen vegetables. They should also come with a user guide.

Imagine if your onboarding materials for a new role included a one-pager about your manager that spelled out things like:

What sorts of decisions are completely for you? When do they want to be consulted, informed or have the final say?

When and how often would they like to hear from you?

When will you be meeting on a regular basis?

What's the best way to get their attention in a hurry?

What are their major triggers or dislikes?

Real talk here for a minute: most bosses probably don't do this. If you're the boss, you can start with your next hire. If you're not the boss, you can ask the questions and assemble your own user guide.

I once figured out that a long-ago boss was terrible at email. He could never seem to get on top of it, so it wasn't an effective way to seek his input on anything meaningful. I learned that the best way to catch him was a quick text message followed by an actual conversation. I had to learn this the hard way, but it wasn't a big deal.

For a later role, I asked my leader a series of questions directly on my very first day. In response, I learned that he had no expectations about my whereabouts or the actual hours I'd work on any given day. And that he'd be happy to provide feedback at any time, but didn't need to hear from me at any given interval.

It was a wonderful relationship that started out right. Kind of like a well-assembled dining room table that can last for years.

Coaching prompts:

- When leading others, what's most important for them to know about how you work?
- Which mysteries about your leader, if you resolved them, would help you be more effective in your own role?

24

◌

The inverted pyramid

"Make me care," said the broadcast journalism professor to the student not yet out of his teens.

The student was me. Decades later, while I remember little else about the class or the professor herself, I remember the punch line. Put your best, most important idea first. Whenever and wherever you're writing anything.

It's a punch line that applies well beyond television news. In leadership, whatever the message and whatever the audience, put first things first. Don't, as we used to say in the news business, "bury the lead."

Picture a pyramid in your mind and turn it upside down. The heaviest, most important part is now at the top. Looking toward the bottom, it gets smaller and lighter until it fades into nothingness. So it should be when you're telling a story.

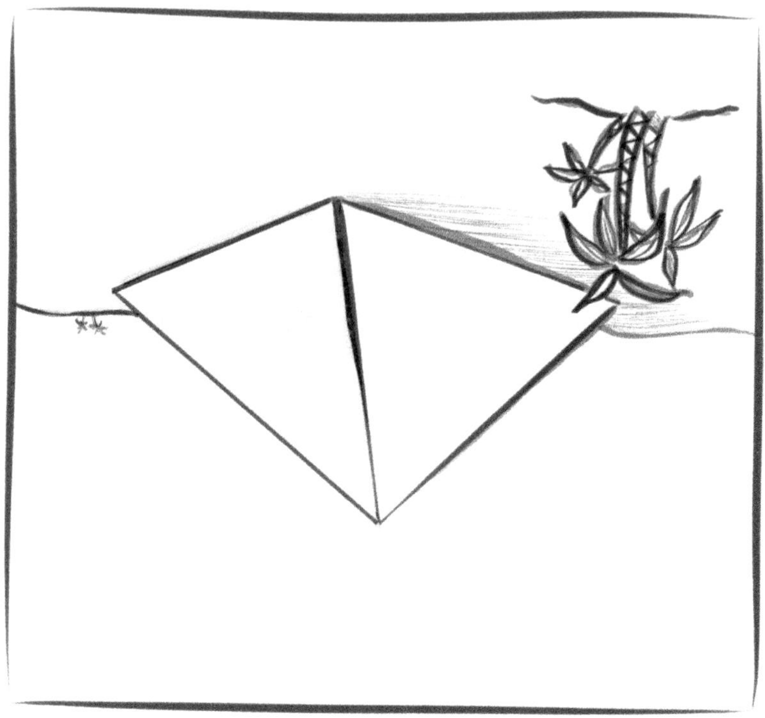

This is a concept that originated with newspapers. Reporters and editors received a designated length for their stories, measured in column-inches, from those who were in charge of laying out the paper. But that length could get shorter, based on ads and other stories. So you wrote your story assuming it would be cut from the bottom up. You made sure the most timely, relevant idea went first, to grab the reader and attract them to the story. You put the less important stuff at the bottom in case it met the red pen.

Newspaper revenues have been declining for decades, but the techniques of those hardworking journalists are as relevant as they ever were. Writing a LinkedIn post? Pitching your boss on adding a position to your team? Describing your company to an investor?

Make me care.

Coaching prompts:

- What is the best, most important, most tangible idea you need to communicate to someone right now?
- What belongs at the bottom of the inverted pyramid, for someone who has more time and interest to devote to what you're sharing?

25

The golden scissors

A chief executive client mentioned that his organization was about to go on a construction spree, because federal dollars had started flowing into infrastructure again.

"We're going to need a lot of golden scissors," he said.

His comment took me back to a time ages ago when the client and I had worked together in government communications.

In my very first job in local government, I worked for an elected official whose entire office was littered with golden scissors. Golden shovels, too. These would fall over on a regular basis, terrifying the receptionist and causing the rest of us to mutter under our breath.

The golden scissors and golden shovels were office clutter. They were also currency.

Elected officials need to take credit for things, because doing so helps keep them in office. And elected officials bring press coverage. Cameras. Publicity.

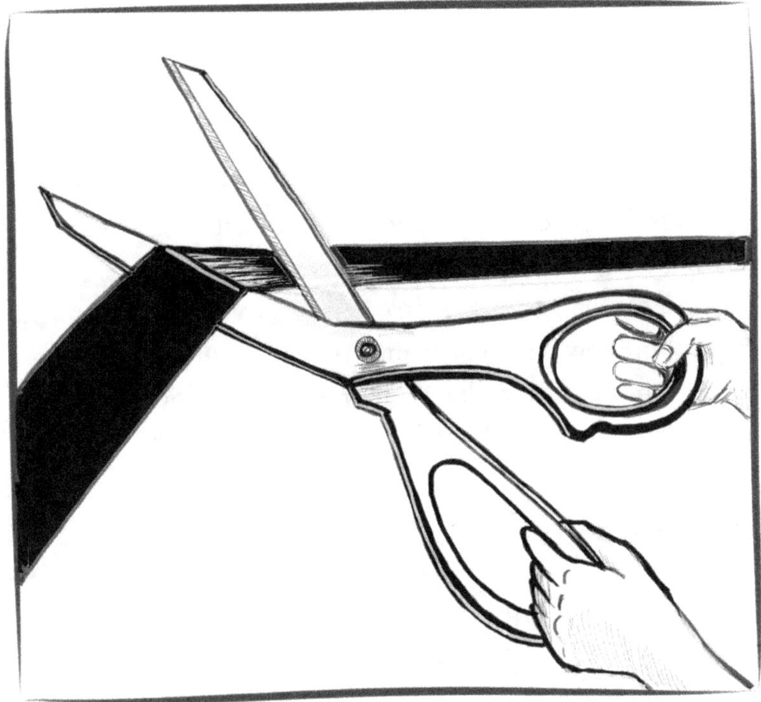

So you'd invite the mayor to your ribbon cutting, even if the mayor had no role in funding, designing or constructing the thing behind the ribbon. Even if the mayor had no awareness of the thing prior to arriving at the ceremony. Even if the mayor had initially opposed the thing.

The facility or infrastructure improvement in question might have been open for weeks already, with the cutting of the ceremonial ribbon tied to the schedule of the most important person who attends. It's all form and no obvious function. And at the end of the event, the ribbon cutters get to keep the scissors.

But this seemingly strange, seemingly silly practice from the world of politics illustrates an important principle in leadership.

It is relatively easy to share credit with others. And to do so often costs next to nothing for the one who is sharing.

In fact, whether it's visibility or goodwill, the person sharing credit usually stands to gain a lot.

You can hand out as many scissors as you like, and make the ribbon as wide as you want. At some point you will run into a limiting factor: the photographer's lens. So it is wise to think about how much credit is too much to share.

Coaching prompts:

- What's one project or initiative for which you can share credit with someone else?
- What do you stand to gain by sharing the credit?

26

∽

Can't sell you the car
at that price

The client was troubled because he couldn't deliver a raise, or a promotion, for a member of his team. The request was off-cycle, and the company leadership was drawing a hard line on new personnel expenses. He had advocated for his employee, but he couldn't get it done. And now he needed to deliver the news.

"I feel like I'm working at a car dealership," he said.

"Tell me more?" I asked, always delighted when a client pops a new analogy into a coaching conversation.

"If I'm a car salesman, sometimes it doesn't matter what I want, or what the customer wants," he continued. "Because sometimes, I just can't sell you the car at that price."

I've never been a fan of the car dealership haggle game. The whole dance seems unnecessarily theatrical, and like a big waste of time. Offer in hand, the salesperson gets up from the desk and slowly shuffles off to the manager's office. There

may be some animated arguing between the salesperson and the manager, for the customer's benefit. The customer may loudly stand up and threaten to leave the dealership. The sequence may repeat itself several times.

This is really how adults are supposed to act toward one another?

It also violates my sense of fairness to think that I might pay less for something than the person next to me, if I can manage to negotiate more aggressively.

But my favorite moment is the one that always arrives at some point. It comes sooner, if the dealer has a no-haggle price posted on its website. Or later, if the negotiation goes on for a few rounds.

If the dealer must sell the car for more than the buyer is willing to pay, there's no deal. My client was at the no-deal moment, and was wringing his hands over how to say it.

"Suppose you switch up your time horizon," I suggested. "And even though you're disappointed you're not going to sell a car that day, you might have another one hit the lot next week that's a better fit for the customer. Or you might be working at a different kind of dealership in a few years and get the opportunity to sell this customer a boat. How would you handle the conversation then?"

The client sighed. He would, he decided, respond with kindness. He'd acknowledge the disappointment all around, without dwelling on his own efforts to close the deal. And he would focus on the relationship in the long term rather than the transaction of the moment.

Coaching prompts:

- How might you deliver unwanted news in a way that strengthens, rather than detracts from, your relationship with the other person?
- What might turn a "no" into a "not now" or "not this" instead?

27

Giving feedback like
a doctor would

"Hi, Alan, it's [redacted], calling about the position at [redacted]."

"Hi, [redacted], great to hear from you! How's it going?" I asked.

"It's going great, thanks. Listen, you haven't got it."

My brain didn't even need to unpack the somewhat distinct verb tense (the hiring manager is Australian). Within five seconds of answering the phone, I had the most important information I needed.

I gathered a bit more detail, learning that my candidacy was strong, but that the person they were hiring was a real star in the field. I thanked him. We made vague plans to get together at some point next time we were near each other. Then the call was over.

I'd invested a lot in seeking this position: flying from California to New York on short notice for an in-person

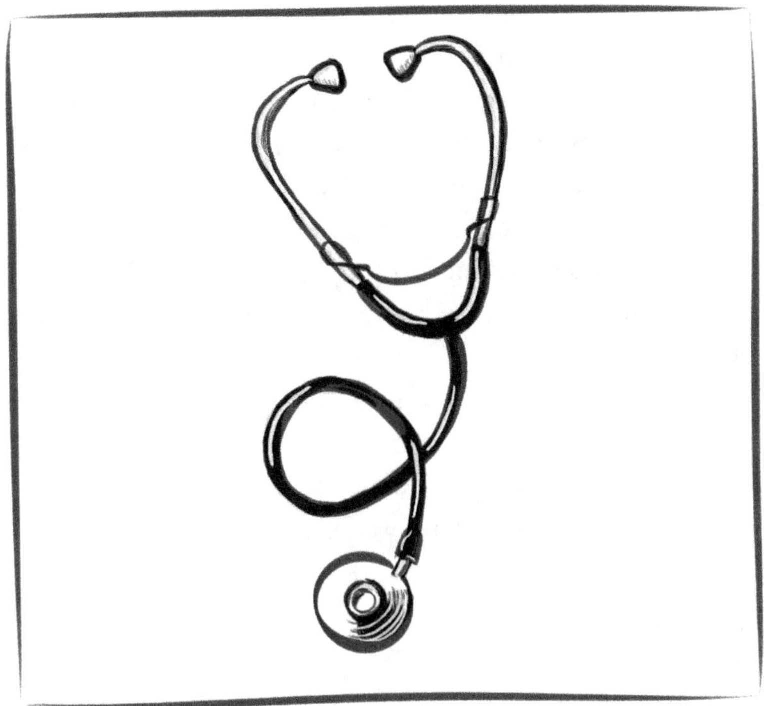

interview, spending half a day with the team I'd be joining, many emails and reference checks. So I was disappointed in the outcome, but the delivery stayed with me.

It struck me that this leader had a rather clinical style of delivering feedback. Not clinical in the sense of cold, harsh or detached. Clinical in the sense of quickly, succinctly and clearly delivering exactly the necessary information. Like a doctor would.

You've waited longer than you'd like for those test results, or for the exam you just had. There are precisely two things you need to know in that pivotal moment.

Is it bad news or good news, and am I going to be OK?

The rest can wait. Yet we're tempted, as compassionate human beings, to craft an artful and lengthy run-up to the key facts. To bury the lead, as we said in journalism school. Imagine how I would feel if my Australian not-to-be-boss called me up and spent 15 minutes talking about how great I was… and then told me I didn't get the job? Or filled the initial conversation with a bunch of technicalities that went over my head?

As of this writing, the conversation happened nearly a decade ago. The hiring manager now runs the organization where I didn't get the job. We never did go out for a beer. And I'm still grateful for his example.

Coaching prompts:

- For the recipient, what is the most important component of the feedback you're about to deliver?
- How can you do this in a way that is digestible, but doesn't unnecessarily soften or delay what you really need to say?

28

The wall doesn't care

My clients tend to be successful people who excel at almost everything they do. I imagine this is because they're good at their jobs, and because they choose roles or projects where success is likely.

Embracing opportunities that bring a possibility of failure is a great way to grow as a leader and as a human being. It's also a painful and unusual thing to do. What I've seen many, many times instead is this: the client brings me a scenario where they've hit a seemingly immovable obstacle.

It just. Won't. Budge. And for the talented fixer of problems, crafter of visions or provider of inspirations, this is a deeply uncomfortable moment.

I had such a call with a client who's a veteran leader in the federal law enforcement space. After decades of personally working, then leading teams of people who work, to keep our nation safe from harm, he's seen some stuff. He's not easily rattled. But this time, he was completely out of ideas.

An employee in his chain of command was safely ensconced in the civil service, just a couple of years away from retirement. This person would make no extra effort, would expend no extra energy beyond the basic minimum to turn in a satisfactory performance evaluation and continue getting a paycheck.

He wouldn't budge. My client had tried everything he knew how to do, everything that had served him well in the past. I had an idea.

"Imagine you put your hands above your head and run screaming into a wall," I said. "Sounds painful, right?"

The client agreed.

"Now, once you've done that," I continued, "does the wall care?"

He chuckled a little. "Nope, the wall doesn't care."

I suggested he might want to have a little chat with himself and do some exploring. Was this situation really worth more of his time and energy? Or, is it possible that he'd finally met his match and it was time to move on?

Frustrating, to be sure. But it would be even more frustrating to keep trying without success until the person finally retired.

Coaching prompts:

- At what point does a problem become intractable and no longer worth trying to solve?
- What does it say about you, and your leadership, if you're facing one of these problems?

29

They brought their own pizza!

"OK, this one *has* to go in your next book," said the client, winding up for a story. He was a chief executive and someone I'd known for more than a decade. He'd been in the job for about 3 years, and had made great strides in creating an open, trusting culture. This was no small feat, given the number of operational and reputational missteps that had sunk his predecessor.

My client was telling me about the annual holiday party. His team had taken pains to create a festive atmosphere, hiring a local vendor for the catering and taking suggestions for the music. He made the rounds, greeting dozens upon dozens of employees and wishing them a happy holiday.

And then he noticed something.

One group of people was sitting off in a corner, glumly keeping to themselves. "Alan," the client said, "they brought their own pizza. To our catered holiday party!"

They seemed determined not to have a good time, and to make sure everyone else noticed. These weren't strangers to the leadership team. They had been agitating loudly during periods of labor-management tension.

How does one react to something like this? "I said hi, and thought about asking for a slice," the client said. "But it wasn't even *good* pizza."

He went on to tell me that he realized some people were never going to be on his side, and he'd reluctantly realized that this was OK. In fact, it was beyond OK. It was necessary. Leadership requires taking risks and making decisions that will meet opposition. Playing it safe will stand in the way of progress, and it won't win everyone over anyway.

So my client said hello to a few more people and then went home to his family. I doubt he's ever looked at pizza the same way again.

Coaching prompts:

- How long do you try to satisfy the needs of a person, or a group, before deciding they won't be satisfied?
- If you knew that a decision would alienate 20 percent of your team, would you make it? What about 50 percent?

Delegation and Developing Others

I have coached people from the head of a dental school to the guy whose team makes sure the warehouse chain has enough frozen pot pies to sell. And not once, in thousands of coaching sessions, do I remember a leader telling me, "Delegation? Yeah, I've got that totally nailed. We don't even need to talk about it."

Delegation is a learned skill. It takes time to figure out, and even more time to do. It requires patience with others and tolerance for mistakes — or even failure. But it's absolutely necessary to free up your time, energy and attention for your most valuable contributions to the organization you're in.

You cannot take a global view of your role if you've got yourself stuck on the ground. And while doing feels good, doers are only successful until they arrive at the gates of leadership. This is why it's so important to hand off the execution swiftly and properly.

A leader's inability to delegate holds others back as well.

If members of the team aren't given the space they need to expand their skills, to take risks, to make mistakes and learn from them, they will either stagnate or leave the organization. Unnecessary turnover is costly and takes a toll on the remaining staff.

It is up to the leader to help develop others, ideally through both direct guidance and creating that space for them to grow.

But the guidance and the space are not enough by themselves. We must remain vigilant about recognizing and eliminating structural barriers to equity at work.

I'm grateful for what seems to be a growing awareness that not all of us have access to the same institutions, relationships and opportunities. Let's continue recognizing that our differences — whether they be mental or physical health, race, gender, sexual orientation or otherwise — do make our workplaces stronger for everyone. And that we should all work to feel empowered to take meaningful action.

In this section, we find ourselves in bathrooms, kitchens, airplanes and other familiar spaces.

30

The president never runs out of toilet paper

Delegation requires trust. It's simple, but not easy. If you don't trust your people, you'll never be able to let go enough for them to do their jobs and for you to do yours. To illustrate this idea, I turn once again to the chief executive of our federal government.

I've asked my clients on occasion to imagine how much trust in staff is necessary for the president to be effective. To me, the office simply doesn't work without it.

For the meeting with a foreign leader to be successful, the protocol experts must prepare just so. The policy experts must make the briefing documents relevant and timely.

For the day to meet its objectives, and to lead to the next effective day, the schedulers must build in time for the president's exercise, meals and rest.

For the news conference to seem thoughtful, the media team must put together photos and bios of the reporters, along with examples of possible questions.

For the speech to have an impact, the writers must revise and rewrite, and the teleprompter operator must keep track of pacing and ad-libs.

And of course, for the comfort and hygiene of the first family and their staff and guests, the bathrooms of the White House must be well-stocked at all times.

The nearest CVS store is about a block away from the White House. But you'll never see the president dashing across 15th Street because someone used the last roll of toilet paper. That's just not the way the job works. And the job works only because of trust.

I imagine a bargain, stated or unstated, that sounds something like this. "I agree to act like the world's most powerful toddler for the next four to eight years, utterly dependent on the lot of you for nearly every single thing I need. And you agree to provide those things, so that together we can make this country a better place."

There's no bargain this grand for the rest of us mere mortals, of course. But smaller, similar bargains abound every day.

Coaching prompts:

- What aspects of your role depend on your ability to trust your staff to do their roles?
- What elements of this kind of trust are hard for you? Why?

31

Loading the dishwasher

If you consider yourself a doer by nature, or you came up into leadership because a technical skill got you promoted, you will likely struggle with delegation at some point.

I'm fond of saying that effective leadership requires being comfortable with an idea that seems completely foreign to an individual contributor: your value to the organization is now delivered, at least in part, through the work of other people rather than your own.

A federal government client was right in the middle of it. He had seemingly endless demands on his time from above, and couldn't get on top of his workload.

Drawing on my finest Homer Simpson, I asked, "Can't someone else do it?"

"I wish," he replied, before laying out the litany of concerns that tend to trip up a wannabe delegator. My people make mistakes, so I'm concerned about the quality. I

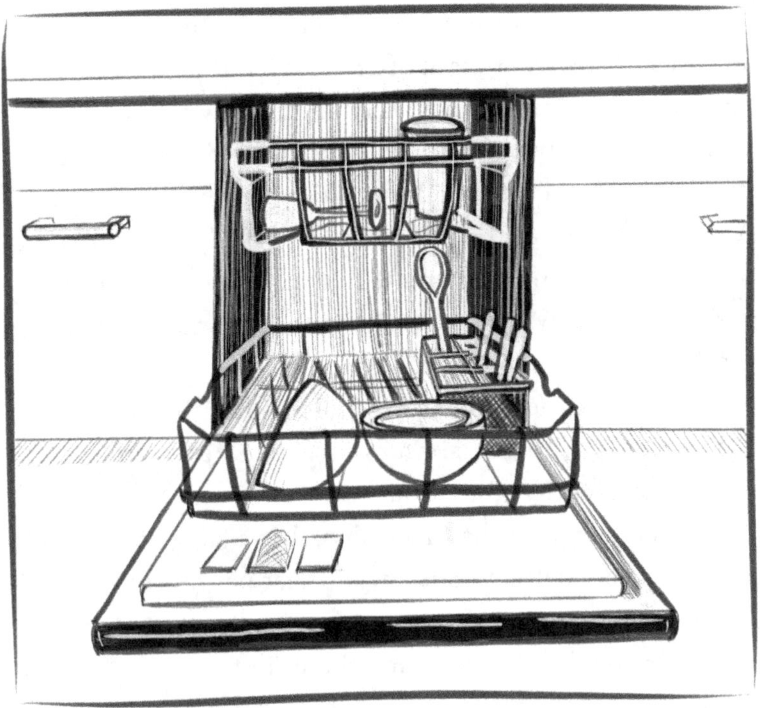

need to step out to teach them how to do things, and I just don't have the time.

I knew my client was a parent, as I am. I also know comparisons of parenting to leadership are fraught with peril, as one doesn't usually fire one's offspring or pay for a direct report's entire college education. But this was worth a shot.

"Think about teaching your kid how to load the dishwasher," I offered.

"Oh… kay?" he replied.

"You know that there's a right way and a wrong way to do it," I continued. "And it's easy to measure success. If you do it right, the dishes come out clean.

"You have a choice. You can keep being the guy who loads the dishwasher night after night. And the dishes *will* be clean. Or you can teach your kid how to load the dishwasher, knowing you're going to have to deal with some dirty dishes for a little while until they get the hang of it.

"What you can't have is both. You can't be resentful that you're the only one who knows how to do the dishwasher right, and be unwilling to work through the messy hassle of teaching your kid how to do it."

He smiled and nodded. We ended our call with him developing a small, initial list of tasks that he would find time to begin delegating to his team.

I'd like to report that my dishwasher analogy cured my client of every delegation issue, and that he was able to cut his working hours by 50 percent. Not so. But he was on his way to feeling like he had some choice in the matter, and was no longer stuck in thinking everything depended only on him.

Coaching prompts:

- What is an area of your work that you'd like to hand off to others on your team?
- How can you provide a safe environment for those team members to learn the task, resisting the urge to aim for perfection until they might be ready?

32

~~~

The CEO flying the plane

Jens Ritter is the CEO of Lufthansa Airlines, the German giant of the skies. He's also a pilot who came up through the ranks of the airline by spending many, many hours in the cockpit. Because he's still type-certified and qualified as a captain, he's legally able to take the helm in about 100 Lufthansa planes.

But. If he actually did this, let's think for a moment about how incredibly odd and unfortunate it would be.

Lufthansa has thousands of pilots. As of this writing, the airline is on a campaign to hire 2,000 new ones. If the CEO is the only person left who can fly the plane, that's either the stuff of a suspenseful film (someone or something knocked out the actual crew) or an operational failure of catastrophic proportions.

From a customer perspective, who delivers the smoother landing: the pilot who does this multiple times every month, or the CEO who does it for the first time in a dozen years?
~~~

While the CEO is tied up in guiding the A340 across the Atlantic for several hours, who is minding his responsibilities and making his decisions? Is the company serving its shareholders by compensating a pilot with a CEO salary?

You don't have to be a CEO (or a pilot) to understand how this idea applies in almost every workplace. The action belongs as low on the org chart as possible. The leader can step in and act as an employee, but an employee can't necessarily step in and act as the leader.

Coaching prompts:

- As the leader, what is compelling you to take a hands-on, operational role instead of leaving it to someone on your team?
- When faced with a challenge you know you can resolve, what happens if you ask yourself, "Am I the best person to do this?"

Postscript: *In 2023, Jens Ritter made headlines (and got his LinkedIn followers talking) by doing a shift as a flight attendant. This undercover boss-style move gave him a fresh perspective on how customers and employees were experiencing their time in the cabin. It's important to note that the perspective shift was the whole point. The CEO refreshes your diet soda not because he's the only person who can do the job, but because he's trying on the role to see it differently.*

33

The CEO and the press release

One of my least favorite memories of running the communications shop for a national nonprofit was the editing process for press releases.

Picture at least a half-dozen people in different areas of an organization, all jumping in with their own attached Word documents with tracked changes, all within minutes of the original draft going out. I always imagined it like hyenas scrambling to feed on a carcass. (This is ironic, because it was an animal protection organization.) And then some poor soul would have to declare the editing window closed, and reconcile all of the different versions that went around.

It was the model of inefficiency, and the reason for the very existence of collaborative word processing software.

But this wasn't the worst part of the process for me.

The worst part of the process was that the CEO himself would line-edit many press releases. He fancied himself

the best writer in the building, having had a version of my job before he had his. He was also exceptionally concerned about accuracy and reputation, to the point of having his #2, my boss, review everything before it went out. A donor, a member of Congress or one of the organization's adversaries might see an error and pick up on it, after all.

The original writer of the press release was at times 6 layers below the big boss on the org chart. The review chain also included those whose subject matter expertise included the topic under discussion.

But all of these trained professionals were not enough to ensure the quality and accuracy of the press release.

The CEO had to do it himself.

Mind you, nobody else in the organization was in a position to do the CEO's job.

If someone were to design a process that would intentionally make multiple layers of thoughtful, committed staff feel basically useless, I couldn't imagine a better way to do it.

And if the CEO truly were the best writer in the building? This was the perfect way to ensure we all depended on him, instead of getting better ourselves.

Coaching prompts:

- To what extent are you taking away the agency, expertise and growth potential of your staff by doing their work for them?
- What are you unable to do yourself as a result, whether setting a vision for the team or other aspects of your role that are uniquely yours?

34

The superhero

When does support of your staff cross the line into overprotecting? When you find yourself being a superhero.

I've had many a client tell me they feel like a human shield for their teams from everything that might descend from above. I had this mindset during a couple of leadership positions of my own. Give me your best work, and I'll protect you from all the crap that nobody should have to deal with except me.

It feels good to be the superhero. You've thwarted the bank robbery, delivered the cat from the tree or kept the freight train from hitting the school bus. The people are thankful!

But there's a giant hole in this approach. When the boss leaves the organization, or goes on vacation, or is just plain unavailable, there's no one left to depend on.

What's missing is the sense of independence that comes from occasionally fighting your own battles, instead of someone else fighting them for you all the time.

Put another way, the near-constant presence of a superhero actually creates a lack of safety, because nobody learns how to rescue themselves from a burning building.

As Kim Scott said in her excellent *Multipliers*, "As leaders, sometimes we are most helpful when we don't help."

Not intervening constantly also has one major benefit for the leader, rather than the team.

Being the superhero is exhausting. Big Head Todd and the Monsters conjured the image of a worn-out crime fighter in their 1997 song "Resignation Superman."

"Yes, he's tired of fighting in this town
All the suffering and vice"
But the bad guys don't have to win if you turn in your cape. Someone else will surely step forward to put it on.

Coaching prompts:

- If you have been shielding your staff, what are some small ways to expose them to challenge or unpleasantness in service of developing their coping skills?
- Think back to a time when you needed to navigate a tricky situation without direct support from your boss. What worked about this situation, and what didn't?

35

Painting the walls

I spend a lot of time on the lower level of our house. It's where my home office sits, and it's where I sit every morning for my daily meditation practice. When I'm in between tasks for my business, or trying to be mindful of my breath, my mind often wanders to a simple but obvious truth: we need to repaint the downstairs.

It's not a visual disaster by any stretch. It's just what happens after 10-plus years of daily use in a family with a pet, and when the walls are a flat white color. Time for an update.

Arranging home-improvement work is one of my least favorite parts of being a homeowner. There's the scheduling headache, the cost, the need to contain the dog for the estimate and the actual work.

Meanwhile, Lindy and I painted all of the walls in our last house. Generally speaking, we know how to do it. Painting over white surfaces wouldn't require priming and

multiple coats either. We could probably get this thing done ourselves with just a few hundred dollars in supplies.

But still, do we really *want* to paint our own house? No. We do not.

Assuming we could set aside the time, there's all the prep work. The taping and tarping and moving furniture. The hauling supplies around. The potential for drips and mess. The cleaning up of the rollers and brushes.

Along with all of that, with our lack of skill and experience, we might be expected to deliver a decent, DIY-quality paint job. One that could take significantly longer to finish as we worked to complete it among our many other priorities in life.

So at some point, we will be hiring professional painters for the lower level. And possibly the upstairs, too.

This is a decision point I faced many times during my work as a leader, and one that my clients face every day as well. When do you paint your own walls, and when do you hire a pro?

It may not seem like a clear-cut decision, as there are advantages on either side. Perhaps there's a cost associated with adding personnel to a project, or it seems like less effort to do it yourself. On the other hand, perhaps the other person really could do it faster and better.

For example, I reached a crossroads a couple of years ago when I decided to hire a bookkeeper. I'm a pretty good bookkeeper myself, and I actually did it as a freelancer early in my career. But I was getting overwhelmed by the mental overhead of switching into bookkeeping mode for a couple hours every week, and then switching back out. I realized this switch wasn't necessary for someone who was in bookkeeping mode for a living, so adding on a couple of extra hours of work at the margin would be easy for them.

Now I get to free up my mind for coaching, facilitating and writing. And my monthly statement reconciliation and expense categorization is in someone else's capable hands.

As for the paint job, we still need to pick a color. But that's probably a different analogy.

Coaching prompts:

- What is the true cost of your doing something that someone else might be able to handle — especially if they could handle it better?
- If you ask for help, what message might that send to those around you on your team? In the rest of the organization?

36

The orthodontist's office

I've spent plenty of time in an orthodontist's office. I never had braces as a kid, but I grew up to be the dad of a daughter who went several rounds with orthodontia. I tend to get a little restless when I'm sitting around, and I'm also naturally curious about how things work.

This is how I discovered that our orthodontist's office is a well-tuned leadership environment. It's designed to consistently make best use of its most valuable resource, which is the time and attention of the orthodontist herself.

Walking through the office takes you past a couple of receptionists and a business manager, tending to the appointments and the insurance and the billing. There might be a detour into a separate room for photography and X-rays. But the bulk of the magic takes place in a big open area with half a dozen stations — each of which has a patient, a parent and a technician.

That's right, an office with one orthodontist can support six patients with appointments at the same time.

The technicians handle all of the tightening and adjusting, the rubber bands, the retainer checks. This process can be quite lengthy. And the orthodontist visits each patient one by one, with a smile and a greeting. She advises the technician and instructs the patient. She might pull the patient and the parent into her office for a discussion of the next treatment plan. And then she moves to the next station.

It's brilliantly efficient and probably very lucrative. It also makes me think about my clients in other leadership environments.

Your staff can manage things effectively, freeing your time and attention for the decisions only you can make. Or they can keep you down in the details for so long that you feel like you're not making any progress.

Be the orthodontist.

Coaching prompts:

- How might you restructure your staffing environment so it supports your agenda as a leader, rather than taking away from it?
- Which elements of your workload might be better accomplished by staffing them out, rather than by doing them yourself?

37

The emergency brake

Decades ago, it was time for my first driving lesson. I remember being nervous when I buckled myself in behind the wheel for the first time. While I don't remember a thing about the instructor, I remember something very specific about the car.

Poking out of the carpet on the passenger side was something that struck me as an abomination. Completely out of context. Like a third wing on a bird or a toilet in the middle of the living room. It was the instructor's emergency brake.

Aesthetic objections aside, the brake was there for everyone's safety. And now that I'm a parent of a teen, I have a very different perspective on it.

Placing a two-ton, potentially lethal weapon into the hands of someone whose prefrontal cortex won't be fully developed for nearly another decade strikes me as a tremendous act of courage.

You can be courageous without being reckless. And this is where the instructor gets to stomp on that pedal and shut the whole thing down.

But when? What are the criteria for using the brake? How does one define, in milliseconds, the line between inconsequential mistakes that all student drivers will make, and mistakes that threaten the car and everyone in it?

As an executive coach rather than a driving instructor, I'm so glad I don't have to answer questions like these. I don't have the stomach for it. But leaders in all organizations face something similar — how far do you let an employee, or a team, go toward failure before you decide to intervene?

You don't want to risk the future of the organization, but you do want them to explore, to learn, even to fail. Your foot may be poised on that emergency brake at all times, or you may want to simply stay vigilant. Even if you're tempted to relegate the student driver to the back seat afterward and drive back yourself, that may not be the right call.

Coaching prompts:

- What value does your work culture place on learning experiences?
- To what extent are you willing to let people make mistakes, in service of their learning?

38

The short doorway

My client was a relatively new hire, into an arts organization that aimed to broaden its worldview. He had upended everything to take the position, moving from a southern state where he had spent most of his life to a city where he'd need to buy his first winter coat.

He was nearly alone as a person of color on the leadership team. He was having trouble figuring out whether his value to the organization was in the decades of experience and deep connections he had within his field, or was a matter of optics, or both. He didn't know how to start that conversation, or if it would be wise not to raise the subject. And he didn't know what else to ask from his supervisor, who was at least coming across as supportive.

"She told me she's always there to hold the door open for me," he said. "Which is great. It's necessary. But I'm not completely comfortable walking through it all the time."

"Well, it seems to me that's because you're 9 feet tall," I said.

The client chuckled, as he had a sense of where I was going.

"She held the door open, and you get to walk through," I continued. "But you're going to have to walk through on your knees, possibly getting your pants dirty and definitely making a scene in the process,"

"I am going to have to do that, yes," he replied.

"Meanwhile, I suspect you might be wondering, 'Where's my light-filled glass atrium already? Where people my size can comfortably stand up straight without attracting a lot of extra attention?' Seems like there's quite a way to go before we get there, no?" I asked.

He agreed. We ended our coaching session with his commitment to imagining that glass atrium and what it would consist of for an organization he really cared about. Ultimately, he decided to stay in the job and continue trying to make a difference.

And he even enjoyed his first snowstorm.

Coaching prompts:

- To what extent does your leadership team encourage, and embrace, points of view that arise from different life experiences?
- What is your organization doing to remove structural barriers to success for employees of underrepresented groups?

39

The junk drawer

The client was a member association executive who was well-regarded and good at her job. Now she'd been handed a struggling part of the organization, with the mission of improving that group's performance and integrating them into the rest of her team.

She was concerned about two things: not knowing the subject matter of the new division as well as her home base, and the pressure to make notable progress early while the CEO was watching.

"It's like dumping out your junk drawer," she said.

Naturally, I had to hear more.

"You've got no idea what's in there," she continued. "Some of it's useful, and some of it probably should have left your house years ago. You can spend hours and hours sorting through it all. But you'd better hurry up because someone's coming over and you've just got a bunch of junk on your kitchen counter."

Sometimes, an image is so vivid that it's instantly relatable. Even the most organized among us have that one spot in our homes. It's where the rubber bands, lint rollers, loose change and expired hand lotion samples almost seem to collect themselves.

Whether it's new or not, a lot of us have that spot in our work lives, too. I asked my client to consider whether the goal was to quickly make the entire drawer spotless, or to bring some order into the picture slowly but visibly.

We talked about quick wins, the ability to solve problems for the new team that were sticky before. We talked about eliminating obvious distractions from the mission. And we talked about pausing after a round of progress, sweeping everything else back into the drawer for a little while and having another go at it later. She resolved to break the process into small pieces instead of trying to tackle it all at once, and to settle into the idea of leaving some of it untackled altogether.

I suspect nobody ever actually gets rid of their junk drawer. If you move to a new house, maybe that stuff will end up in a box before it migrates to a new drawer. Or maybe it will just accumulate again, attracting more odds and ends over time.

Coaching prompts:

- If you have a persistently messy situation at work, what's one thing you could do to make a visible impact on it?
- What's a potential advantage of leaving some of the messiness unresolved?

40

The left-handed scissors

I was in the car, listening to another episode of Morra Arons-Mele's excellent "Anxious Achiever" podcast about mental health and leadership, when something her guest said stopped me cold. I had to go back and listen to it again.

Human resources leader Clayton Lord was explaining what it's like to be in the world with a neurodiversity — or what some younger folks call being "neuro-spicy."

Lord was describing how thoughtful he needed to be in interacting with colleagues when he joined the team at a new organization.

"I have been very conscious about engaging the way I have learned how to engage, which I don't think of as a negative at all. Sometimes I'm in conversations with folks and they say things like, 'Oh, that must be so hard,' or whatever. And it's not really that it's hard, it is that it's something I need to think about. But it's something I need

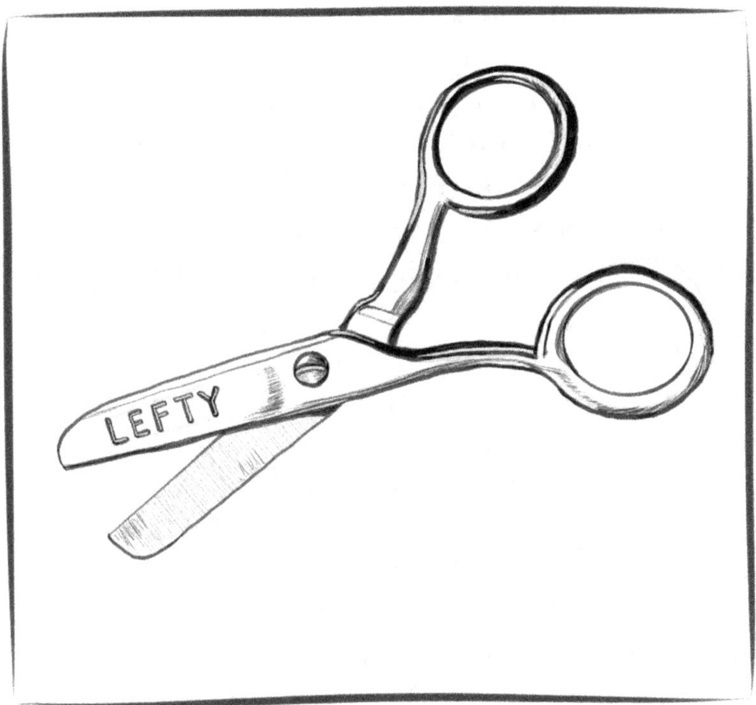

to think about the way that I'm left-handed and I need to think about using right-handed scissors. Like, that's just the way the world is, and you can be upset about it or not."

Lord's analogy landed with me not because I have a neurodivergence, but because in daycare and elementary school, I was the kid with the scissors.

I was the kid who needed to stop the action and fish through the bin to find the scissors with the green handles. If I found them before the couple of other lefties in my class did, they might be rusty or gunky. They probably didn't cut very well. And my classmates would get annoyed at the interruption because they just wanted to start the art project.

A few years later, my adaptation was to teach myself to cut right-handed. I would barely think about it after a while, and I haven't held a pair of green-handled scissors in many decades. I suppose this might have been a bigger challenge if my job ever involved cutting fabric or paper on a regular basis.

My late grandfather was left-handed at a time when such a thing was seen as an aberration. Kids his age were forced to conform to right-handedness, under penalty of punishment. When I was younger, I thought it was really neat that he could write pretty well with both hands. But now, I can't imagine what it must have been like for him to get to that point.

What I took from Clayton Lord's interview is that adaptations can be onerous or they can be a worthwhile challenge. But I'm glad we are living in a generation when discussing them — and all that they require — is out in the open more than it's ever been.

Coaching prompts:

- When something sets you apart from your colleagues, what is the cost of masking that attribute instead of leaning into it? What opportunities would leaning in present?
- If you are managing someone whose identity differs from yours in some way, what support do they need most to be successful? How can you best provide that support?

SECTION 5

Career Progress and Transitions

I'm writing these words in mid-2024, recovering from what might be my first bout of COVID-19. It felt like a few days of a pretty bad cold. It's hard to believe this was a variant of the same virus that caused so much loss of life, livelihood and learning just a few years ago.

The pandemic really scrambled the working world, with consequences we're still trying to figure out. Remote work was impossible until it was necessary. Now it's… occasionally to always good? Record numbers of people have left the employment universe to work for themselves.

Multiple careers are the norm, not the exception. Career paths often look like the robot vacuum squiggle path I wrote about in my last book, rather than anything resembling a straight line or even an arc.

This is a lot of change. But change doesn't have to be as hard as we think it is, and we often have more choice than we realize. I know this in part from personal experience.

I resigned from eight jobs and was fired from two before I started my own business. Since then, I've guided numerous clients through career redesigns — including those who hired me specifically for that reason, and those who came to the conclusion during a regular coaching engagement that it was time to hit the road.

How can you tell you're making progress in your own career, or that you're helping others on your team make progress in theirs? What makes a career transition worthwhile, or effective? Read on.

41

Swing at that ball!

I was talking with June (not her real name), a client who was excelling at every assignment — especially the ones that had nothing to do with her job description. She was performing at a level above her title and pay grade. We talked about what it might look like to close the gap between her work and her compensation.

This was an uncomfortable subject. June saw herself as the sort of employee who would always deliver 110 percent. Who would keep her head down and get the job done. And for whom opportunities would arise because others would notice how hard and how well she was working.

Yet she'd reached a juncture that was very familiar to me. I'd been there, as had many of my clients. Her work no longer spoke for itself. The work hadn't changed, but the environment had. Leadership was too busy to notice how impressive her efforts were. She'd have to advocate for herself.

An opportunity arose.

June's immediate supervisor was on track for a promotion as the department was being restructured. June had offered her full support in a recent conversation. That's when the supervisor had extended an invitation: book some time in a couple of weeks, and let's talk about your career plans here.

Yet she was still hesitant to ask for what she wanted, what she felt she deserved.

"June," I said. "Your boss just lobbed an easy serve over the net. Are you going to take a swing at it, or not?"

She paused to ponder.

"I could," she responded. "I could come up with a revised job description and bring it in there, and see what she thinks."

I invited June to consider the risks of action versus inaction in this situation. She'd be exposing some ambition, sure. But would the promotion be at all likely without doing so?

She decided she would take the swing in their next one-on-one meeting.

Coaching prompts:

- In what ways might advocating for yourself benefit others in various directions on the organizational chart?
- When allies for your career ambitions present themselves, what do you do to recognize and embrace the opportunity?

42

〜⟁

Don't wait until the
building's on fire

The client was a longtime law-enforcement leader in the federal government, a couple of years shy of being eligible to retire. He came into his session wanting to develop some steps to explore what a new career direction might look like. I wasn't surprised, but I was curious about why this was a topic for now.

He mentioned some organizational changes, including the possibility that he might be asked to move across the country in the next few months. This was a nonstarter given his family situation.

Then he asked if he could tell me a quick story. (I never say no to this.)

Law enforcement and public service ran deep in his family, my client explained, and he'd gotten to know more than a few firefighters as a result.

"They have this thing they'll do in certain areas," he said. "They'll go in and visit a local manufacturing business, introduce themselves and take a walk around inside.

"It's good for community engagement, but it helps them in their work too. They make note of where the chemicals are, where the exits are, and pass that information along at the station. You don't want to figure these things out when the building's already on fire, because those few seconds can help keep a firefighter alive."

I understood where my client was going here. Job security, even in the federal government, isn't what it used to be. Better to know where the exit is when you're able to find it on your own.

I asked him which initial steps would be helpful to start his exploration, knowing he had at least a few months to prepare. He resolved to check in with a few colleagues who were facing a similar situation, and to check out a few asynchronous learning options that would get him headed toward a possible second career.

We ended our call with the makings of a plan. I told him I appreciated how he remained open, thoughtful and calm during a time that was probably very stressful.

Coaching prompts:

- What would help you prepare for an unexpected change in your career direction? Who can support you in this preparation?
- Under what circumstances do you think you'd no longer be able to do the job you're in now?

43

Key in the lock

The pin-tumbler lock is an engineering marvel dating back to President Lincoln's time, and one that's still in wide use today. The basic idea: the ridges in the key move the pins into place. If the pins are all aligned, the key can turn and the lock will open.

Plenty of keys will slide into that lock. But it takes a very specific cut to open it. And sometimes a key stops working, because it wasn't cut well or because dust is getting in the way inside the lock.

In leadership, you've probably slid that key into the lock hundreds of times. You've turned it without thinking about it. Then, one day, it sticks.

A new boss, a reorganization or even a different strategic plan can scramble the pins or deposit some gunk inside.

It's uncomfortable, but it doesn't have to be nasty or personal. Sometimes the key just doesn't open the lock anymore. The fit with a leader, or an organization, is a very

individual thing. What works for others may not work for everyone, so it's possible you're no longer working in an environment that suits you.

How to minimize discomfort and keep your career on track? Notice the friction. If it used to be easy to have certain conversations or to make certain moves, is it now more difficult?

If you've blown away the dust, lubricated the lock and tried a different key, and the tumbler still won't turn, perhaps someone has changed the lock without telling you. Then it's about time to find a door you can actually open again.

Coaching prompts:

- In what ways are you able to adapt to changing circumstances around you at work?
- What sorts of changes make you uncomfortable, and why?

44

Your job is your home

On a given weekday, many of us will spend more time on work than on anything else while we're awake. Regardless of whether you work at home, work is a home, for your professional aspirations, income needs and connections with other people.

Here are three mini analogies on the work-as-home theme.

The condo

Woe to the newly-promoted executive who believes they can take on all of their new responsibilities by just working longer and harder — for more than a brief ramp-up period. You have to realize at some point that you're just one person with limited capacity. Better to anticipate this early than to discover it once you're already in burnout mode.

I had a client who was preparing to make a leap like this. She'd always worked hard, and was preparing to work harder. In the interest of her success in the long term, I asked her to imagine moving into the new role as moving house.

"Let's say you're moving from your nice big house in the suburbs into a really, really expensive condo downtown," I said. "It doesn't matter how fancy your new place is, or how much you paid for it. You will still never, ever be able to fit all of your old furniture in there. You want to get the most out of your investment, so everything you bring with you or buy new has to be truly important."

By the end of that call, we'd already begun exploring which meetings, projects and responsibilities wouldn't fit into her new role.

The keys

A client and I were talking about the awkward stage that sometimes happens on the way out the door of a job. He had given notice and was getting ready for a new role in a new organization. In the final days of his existing position, he had already handed off most of his responsibilities and was finding himself with less and less to do.

Still, he was a current employee who was still getting paid. He still cared about the place, and he still had obligations to fulfill — like exit interviews and giving back his laptop.

"It's like you've already moved out," he said, "but you haven't quite handed in the keys."

The stage is awkward, but very temporary. The lease will end, the last day on the job will come. Eventually, someone else will take over the space.

The former residence

I've left ten jobs since graduating from college. Among my former staffers who moved on, and clients I've coached through career transitions, I count dozens if not hundreds of people.

Not a single one of us has cared as much about a position or a workplace after leaving as we did when we were in it. This decline in caring isn't immediate. It can take a little time, and it can be painful, but it always, always happens.

One of my clients was preparing to make their transition out of a long, long employment relationship. They were so steeped in their own role, and the entire organization's history and growth, that they couldn't imagine caring less.

I asked them to think back to the last time they moved out of a house or apartment.

When you spend a lot of time in a place, you get to know the ins and outs almost without thinking about them. The toilet flush handle that needs an extra jiggle once in a while. The one plant in the garden that always needs extra water because it gets so much sun.

But when you move out, these are someone else's concerns. You might occasionally wonder how that plant is doing, or even see it from the road if you're back in your old neighborhood. It's just not part of your responsibilities anymore.

Whether you're replaying toxic memories and relieved not to be repeating them, or wondering about the team's progress on the project you didn't get to finish, these thoughts will come up. They'll lessen eventually.

Your colleagues might call you for advice once a day, or not at all. You don't have to wonder about this, and you don't have to answer if you don't want to.

It's just not your house anymore.

Coaching prompts:

- When you're moving into a new position in the same organization, what elements of your old work will you need to let go of to be successful?
- What can you do to remind yourself that moments of career transition, while potentially sticky or emotional, are always temporary?
- Which responsibilities or relationships will be the easiest to leave behind when you change jobs? Which will be the hardest, and why?

45

The warm bed

Restlessness in a job or a career shows up differently for different people. It could be a growing sense of boredom, a lack of fulfillment. Or it could even be a feeling of comfort, as a client brought into one of our sessions.

"I feel like this job is sort of like a warm bed these days," she said. "I'd love to lie around in here all day, but how do I know when it's time to get up?"

I appreciated the image from the moment she named it. For starters, no leader has ever told me they get enough high-quality sleep. Also, in the winter where I live, you wake up when it's dark outside and realize you've already just had the warmest moment of your day.

If you're physically and mentally well, you can't stay in bed all day, every day. You'll miss out on the interactions and opportunities the outside world has to offer. The dog won't be able to walk herself. And you won't be able to take care of

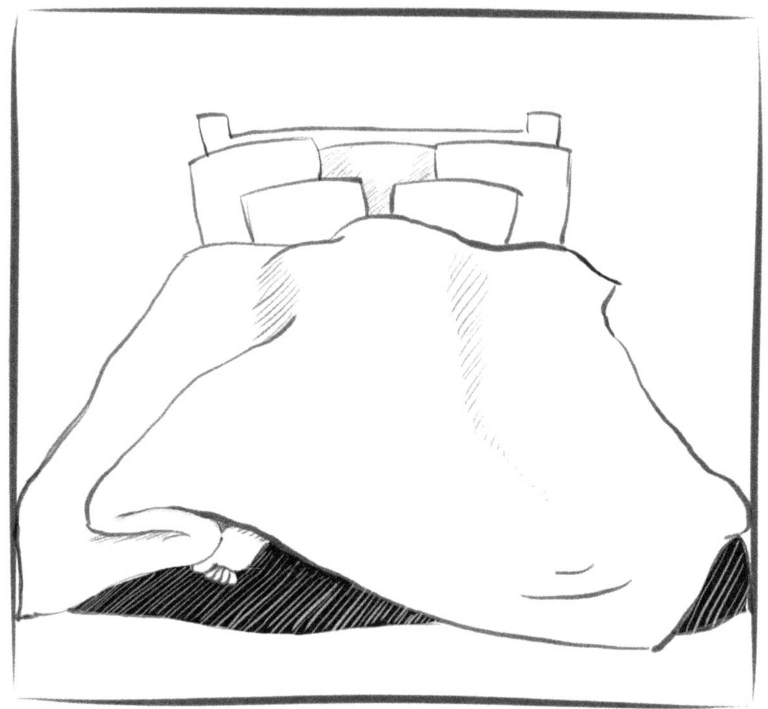

your many bodily needs lying down. There will come a point in time when you simply need to get vertical again.

What if that point in time isn't so obvious as the blare of an alarm clock or a signal that you have to pee? How do you figure it out?

For starters, consider when it's not the right time. You might wake up in the middle of the night from a nightmare or a stiff shoulder, look at the clock and realize you're not done sleeping for a few more hours. At work, you may not yet feel a sense of completion on a program, an initiative or a key hire. You may also have a feeling of equilibrium in your daily routine or your family life. You may have created space for non-work priorities. All of these elements may signal that it's not yet time to go.

If the comfort you're experiencing becomes a dull annoyance, or if you're yearning to discover what else is out there in the world, that's a different kind of signal worth at least a little curiosity.

Coaching prompts:

- In what ways have you worked to develop a feeling of comfort in your position, and how is that comfort serving you?
- How might your feeling of comfort be holding you back?

46

The root-bound plant

Potted plants are not always easy to keep happy. It takes the right combination of light, watering and potting mix to make a container plant thrive — like creating a small ecosystem that nature can't provide. Done right, you've added texture and color to indoor spaces, porches or balconies. Done wrong, you've got droopy leaves or "I'm just not good with plants."

The size of the pot matters, too. Get all of the other conditions right, and you're likely to face a root-bound plant at some point. It's stuck. Can't grow any bigger, because its natural state of pushing outward has reached an artificial limit in the form of its plastic or ceramic container. The roots are growing through and around one another, and eventually they won't be able to absorb what the plant needs to continue thriving. If it suddenly seems to need more water every day, that's a good clue. The attentive gardener then faces a choice.

You can untangle the root ball and trim some of it away. Perhaps some of the foliage, too. If you're careful, you'll now have a happy potted plant again. Or you can invest in an even larger pot with even more soil and nutrients. Then you're likely to have a happy, larger potted plant. Eventually, you'll end up with a pot so large that it might be quite expensive — and require a friend to help you move it around.

It's true that some plants thrive in root-bound conditions. It takes a little stress to get them to bloom, or the snugness of the container helps them grow. But this is the exception, not the rule.

In the working world, we've all come across unhappy potted plants from time to time. They're among our co-workers, our team members and perhaps even ourselves. A careful leader notices that someone on the team seems to have become root-bound. A thoughtful conversation with that employee might reveal a desire for growth. If the person is looking for a larger, more complicated challenge, a promotion into a larger pot might be in order. The leader and the employee work together on the transition from individual contributor to new manager, for example.

But promotions aren't for everyone, and neither is the craft of leading people. Sometimes the answer is to create better conditions within the existing container. The leader and employee might prune back some responsibilities or some old aspirations that just don't fit the role anymore. The objective isn't necessarily growth, but helping the person find more comfort and fulfillment in the space they already occupy.

Careful leaders don't let members of their teams simply wither. If someone needs more attention than usual or seems to have droopy as a default state, it's probably time to check on the size and shape of their pot.

Coaching prompts:

- What does development look like for each member of your team? How can you help them meet their aspirations?
- As a leader, which obstacles to success can you remove for others?

47

Air Force One stuck in the mud

The client was the head of an academic institution, a role he'd held for just a few months but had done at two other schools in the past. He was pretty unflappable, but today he was visibly rattled. His pen sliced through the air as he gestured his way through his latest challenges.

He felt that his role as a change agent and his plans to set a sustainable course for the future were at risk, he explained, because of forces that seemed to be beyond his control. Bureaucracy, tradition, inertia, perhaps employees in the wrong jobs, were making almost everything take longer than he wanted it to take. From something as complicated as reorganizing a department to something as simple as ordering a new chair, it all left him stymied and feeling pretty helpless.

The danger, my client realized, was that he wouldn't be able to fulfill everyone's expectations of him as a leader. From his staff on up to his boss, everyone was counting on him to improve things his predecessors could not. He had a one-on-one scheduled with his chairperson the next day, and was grappling with how much of his struggle to reveal.

We talked through various possibilities. Say too little, and the expectations might continue unfulfilled. Say too much, and he risked laying all of his problems at someone else's feet. He landed on asking his boss, who had worked with him at a previous employer as well, for some guidance on how to help move the obstacles or work through them.

After our call, I remembered something from my distant career past.

When I was a young television reporter in downstate Illinois, then-President Clinton had wrapped up a visit to our media market when his plane got stuck in the mud. One of the wheels had come just a little bit off the pavement at the small Urbana airport, and the jet could go no further. Of course, this made national news, and some of my colleagues got to cover the story. The airport was closed for several hours as a backup plane arrived for the president and the press, and workers eventually freed the original.

Jokes about the trajectory of Clinton's presidency aside, I think there's a lesson here. Air Force One is the stuff of legend and the subject of a Harrison Ford movie. It has some of the most advanced communications equipment, a kitchen, sleeping quarters and a medical staff on board. And for all of this sophistication, it is sometimes no match for a simple, sticky substance that's been around for millions of years.

Sometimes, in other words, we just get stuck in stuff.

Coaching prompts:

- What unexpected obstacles have challenged you in your leadership?
- How do you understand the distinction between your own limitations and external factors that can make you less effective?

48

Don't hide the ladder

ere's a frequent topic for a coaching session, or even an entire coaching engagement: a leader is puzzled about why they're not advancing in their organization.

We can, and do, talk about executive presence and political savvy and all of the things that ambitious folks are supposed to bring to the table at work. And I will often get curious about something else that could be at play.

Sometimes, your supervisor isn't being fully candid about the path to promotion in your organization, or the fact that there isn't one in your case.

In other words, they're hiding the ladder.

Imagine trying to climb upward in a completely dark room that's also full of furniture. You suspect there might be a ladder in there somewhere, so you feel around. You bump into things. You trip and fall. Perhaps your patience is rewarded and you find your way to the rungs, or perhaps you give up and leave the room.

If you're the leader, it's your job to turn on the lights.

I know this firsthand, because I was once in a leadership position and completely in the dark during my search for my own ladder.

The person I originally reported to had retired, leaving me with many of his responsibilities and all of my original remit, too. I had some questions. Would I be promoted? If so, what did the path look like, and how long might it take? Or would they backfill his position?

I wanted answers. I requested them frequently for several months, either in my weekly one-on-ones with my boss or my rare hallway conversations with the CEO. But the answers never came. My questions were deflected, or I was thanked for my patience and cooperation while "we need to figure some things out."

If I'm being charitable to these two executives, I suspect they didn't know the answers. Or perhaps they had priorities more pressing than figuring out the answers or sharing them. In the meantime, I was effectively doing what were two people's jobs for less than half the price.

The bottom line was that the ladder didn't exist, so I never found it. What I eventually found instead was the exit.

There are plenty of reasons someone might not find themselves on the upward trajectory. Some of these are perfectly legitimate (limited number of leadership positions, limited turnover, limited skills or perspective), and some are not (racism, patriarchy, "We really need you in your current role.")

If you are aware of these reasons and don't have enough influence to change them, part of your duty as a supervisor is to share what you know.

If there's a ladder, don't hide it. If the ladder doesn't exist, don't pretend that it does.

Coaching prompts:

- What is the path to growth or promotion for each of the employees you supervise? If you're unclear on the answer, what would it take for you to get to clarity?
- If an employee doesn't have a path to growth or promotion, but wants one, how comfortable are you in having that conversation?

49

Natural foods co-op vs. the military

In our young vegan days in the early aughts, Lindy and I would find our way most weekends into a natural-foods co-op just outside DC. It was the sort of place that looked largely unchanged since its founding in the late 1960s. Think wooden crates and bulk bins stacked up to the ceiling. A manual-entry cash register. And a particular smell that reminded me of vitamins, dried herbs and incense all mixed together.

This place wasn't just unusual because you could fill your own container with bulk peanut butter (and would be expected to wash the spoon). It was also a worker-owned cooperative. Most of the employees we encountered were cheerful, talkative, and yes, pretty blissed out. Nobody was in a hurry. The co-op was a place to stock up on tempeh, but also a nice change from our own hard-charging careers in education and nonprofit management.

No one is the boss because everyone is the boss. It's a nonprofit where extra revenue is invested into the store or into the community. The lights have to stay on, and there has to be enough money to keep the shelves stocked, but the money itself isn't the goal.

I haven't been inside that co-op in years, but I think about it often when I'm working with clients who come to me for support in their career transitions. An early step in that process is to take a deep look at what's working in their current or most recent job situations — and what isn't.

"When you think of the type of environment that helps you thrive at work," I might ask, "Do you think of something more like a natural foods co-op, or like the military?"

I freely admit to my clients that I'm prone to exaggerating for the sake of illustration. (The book you have in your hands, and the one that came before it, have dozens of examples of this tendency.) In reality, not many people I work with would choose either option. But they would choose a point on a scale between the two and make it a focal point in their search.

If you want to follow clear directions, to have no ambiguity around who's in charge and why, to understand clearly what success looks like because someone has spelled it out, you're going to want to work at a hierarchical and highly structured organization.

If you want to find your own way, to work collaboratively with others, to chart your own path to success, an organization with a flatter structure or even a holacracy is going to be a better bet.

Just don't forget to wash the spoon.

Coaching prompts:

- What is the role of structure in your personal formula for career success? Are you the sort of employee who thrives in a heavily structured environment or tends to push back against it?
- Do you find it more appealing to have a path that is defined for you or a path that you discover and define as you go?

SECTION 6

～⌒

About Coaching

What is coaching? What do coaches do, and how does the process work?

I'm a big believer in the coaching process, starting with my first turn as a client more than a decade ago. In the time since, I'm so glad that the profession has gained a lot of awareness and momentum. It's rare that I meet someone at a happy hour or on an airplane who's never heard of executive coaching.

This gives me the opportunity to go into a bit more depth, especially when I'm talking to a prospective client.

Here is how I describe what I provide:

I create space for you to talk about work things that you either feel like you can't talk about with anyone else, or that perhaps would be unwise to talk about with anyone else. I listen, inquire, reflect back. I ask questions that reframe your situation in your mind, helping you to see it differently.

Ideally, seeing it differently leads to different actions. Different actions lead to different behaviors. Different behaviors lead to different habits. And different habits lead to different outcomes — filtering all the way through the teams the leader looks after.

It is a path to systems change, starting with a safe and confidential space for the client.

The last three analogies in this collection are about the coaching space and what it makes possible.

50

I see a lot of shoulders

It was a weird, frustrating medical phenomenon. With a combination of physical therapy, massage and time, I'd recovered from a frozen shoulder. But several months later, more suddenly and painfully, my *other* shoulder froze.

So there I was again, in the office of an upbeat and personable orthopedic surgeon, describing my symptoms and complaining that it was hard for me to sleep.

We did range-of-motion tests, and he administered a cortisone shot directly into the muscle. I didn't watch, and it wasn't painful. But it's an eerie sensation to feel something traveling that far into one's body and back out again. I'm sure it was a very long needle.

The whole situation was just profoundly odd to me. So, as I was putting my shirt back on and pondering another series of PT exercises, I asked the doctor to hang back for a moment.

"This doesn't bother you at all, the fact that I can't raise my arm up over my head?" I asked. "And the fact that nobody knows why this happens?"

"I see a lot of shoulders," he replied. "You'll be fine."

It's a phrase that comes back to mind often when I'm coaching leaders. I think it to myself when a client brings me the latest tale of an underperforming employee, or an unreasonable boss, or an unpopular decision.

In a way, I see a lot of shoulders too.

Not that I'm dispassionate about my clients' issues. Or that it's my job to diagnose something wrong and try to fix it like a doctor would. Rather, I like to offer my clients the occasional reassurance that they're not the only person in the world to whom this unfortunate thing is happening right now. Sometimes there's comfort in knowing you, or your circumstances, aren't unique.

In coaching school, we are often warned not to lean too hard on our own opinions. That's what consultants and mentors do. But our opinions do help our clients at times, especially if we offer them lightly and without judgment.

By the way, the good news is that my second frozen shoulder resolved itself over time as well. I'm feeling great and have full range of motion.

Coaching prompts:

- Is the situation you're facing right now so unusual, or so complex, that nobody else could possibly share it or understand it?
- If you found someone in a similar situation, what would you advise them to do or say?

51

Unexploded ordnance

One of Washington, DC's most prestigious neighborhoods is home to American University, a well-known hospital, numerous embassies and even more private residences. In a true calamity of urban planning, the place was also a U.S. Army testing ground for biological weapons during World War I.

More than 100 years later, the Army Corps of Engineers says the cleanup of Spring Valley is all but complete. For years, a homeowner or utility crew would dig up a backyard only to find something very old, potentially explosive and definitely dangerous.

I was tangentially connected to this situation through my work many jobs ago, so I got to learn a lot about unexploded ordnance. (Side note: the difference between "ordnance" and "ordinance" got hammered into my head during journalism school. So we won't be talking about local government laws here.)

Here's something that fascinated me at the time and still does. Let's say someone uncovers a mustard gas shell during a landscaping project. The Army Corps can't leave it in place. They can't take it far away, because transporting these explosives across state lines is risky and also illegal. So the safest, most prudent thing is actually to blow it up somewhere nearby.

So the federal government built a detonation chamber nearby to do just that. In a fancy residential neighborhood with a hospital, a university and embassies in it. With the amount of local pressure involved, you'd best be sure that chamber was airtight and as soundproof as possible.

I think about that detonation chamber sometimes during sessions with my coaching clients. Sometimes, leaders are digging around in their minds during the course of their ordinary work and find something unfamiliar. It could be harmful. They don't want it to blow up right in front of them, and they don't want to endanger others who might be around.

Say you've discovered that you have designs on someone else's position at work. Or that you'd like to explore taking your career in a different direction. Toss these potentially explosive thoughts into the safe container of a coaching session and see what happens. You may end up dispersing a poisonous set of thoughts by talking through them. You may end up with something worth investigating further. Or the whole thing might turn out to be a dud.

Coaching prompts:

- What's one idea in your mind that feels scary or unfamiliar right now?
- In what way might it be helpful to have a safe space to talk through that idea?

52

Turn the camera around

You slip your phone out of your pocket, and point it in the direction of something that caught your eye. It's a bird! It's a plane! It's a silly billboard! And then, you notice that you're not looking at your future cherished memory on your screen. You're looking at a bemused, slightly out-of-focus version of your own face.

Turns out your phone was in selfie mode. I'm sure it's happened to everyone at some point, even though we've only had widespread access to the technology for 15 years or so.

Once I get past the inevitable "Gah, that's not what I wanted! I don't need a picture of myself" moment, I try to remember to pause and see if I can notice anything important.

Are my glasses dirty? Is there something in my teeth?

It's possible that I get so wrapped up in looking at my own reflection that I forget what I was trying to photograph in the first place. Or the moment passes.

The unexpected selfie is exactly what I deliver for my coaching clients: a different, possibly novel perspective. One that's focused entirely on you.

Clients often come into coaching because they are searching for a new perspective. They're feeling stuck or locked into a point of view. Instead of giving them the answers or telling them what they should do, my role is to call up their best from within so they can find the answers.

One of the best ways to do this is reframing. I can help you cast your stories, obstacles and situations in a different light by looking at them differently.

It is the coach's job to help you turn the camera around.

Coaching prompts:

- How might your perspective on a situation change if you took a moment to look away from the situation, and looked at yourself instead?
- What would others say if they were observing you in the same situation?

Author's Acknowledgments

I'd like to extend my gratitude to the several hundred coaching and facilitation clients who have placed their faith in me during their leadership journeys. I am so fortunate to be able to ride alongside such talented, curious, thoughtful leaders.

To A, D, J, J, J, P, S, S, T and W for trusting me as your coach, and for your contributions to this collection of analogies.

To Laura and Jessica, for becoming the ancestors-in-spirit of my coaching practice way back in 2014.

To Dennis, for bringing my second cover to life on the first try, and for our occasional collaboration spanning more than a decade.

To Maura and Andrea, for bringing polish and professionalism into making this project ready for the world. And to Amruza for the thoughtful pre-read that led to some much-needed structural changes.

To Jennifer, Deepti and Rachael for being the world's best collaborators a self-employed coach and facilitator could imagine.

To Xiao Ya, for providing me with plenty of material for a second book, and for always carrying her phone and a few bandages.

To Lindy, my partner in life, in parenting and occasionally in work, for knowing how to express my ideas better than I do.

And to you, the reader, for investing your energy and attention in my work.

About the Author and Illustrator

Alan Heymann is an executive coach, facilitator, speaker and author. He specializes in helping his fellow introverts discover their superpowers, and in supporting leaders through career transitions. Through his business, Peaceful Direction, Alan has worked with clients born in 32 countries. His clients have spanned corporations (including the Fortune 50); nonprofit organizations; public utilities; and federal, county and municipal governments.

Alan spent more than two decades in public, government and nonprofit communications, leading teams of people who use words and images to inspire positive change in society.

He holds a Bachelor of Science in Journalism from Northwestern University, a Juris Doctor from The George Washington University Law School and an Executive Certificate in Leadership Coaching from Georgetown University.

Alan is on the Board of Trustees of the Barker Adoption Foundation, has followed a plant-based diet since 2002 and enjoys running half-marathons. Alan and his family live in Maryland.

Embrace Your Inner Peaches is his second book.

Lindy Russell-Heymann has more than two decades of experience in education and the arts. She began her career as a theatrical costume designer before becoming a teacher. She is a winner of the "Power of Art" award from the Robert Rauschenberg Foundation.

Lindy has a Bachelor of Fine Arts from DePaul University and a Master of Arts in Art Education from The Ohio State University. She's followed a plant-based diet since 2002 and enjoys working with stained and fused glass. She and her family live in Maryland.